Country Ways *and* Country Days

From Weathervanes and Tractors to Auctions and Outhouses . . . Remembering Rural Life

Jerry Apps

Voyageur Press

Library of Congress Cataloging-in-Publication Data
Apps, Jerold W., 1934-
  Country ways and country days : from weathervanes and tractors to auctions and outhouses--remembering rural life / Jerry Apps.
      p. cm.
  Rev. ed. of: Symbols. c2000.
  Includes bibliographical references (p. 173) and index.
  ISBN-13: 978-0-89658-717-5
  ISBN-10: 0-89658-717-7
  1. Chain O' Lakes Region (Wis.)--Social life and customs--20th century--Anecdotes. 2. Farm life--Wisconsin--Chain O' Lakes Region--Anecdotes. 3. Material culture--Wisconsin--Chain O' Lakes Region--Anecdotes. 4. Apps, Jerold W., 1934---Childhood and youth--Anecdotes. 5. Chain O' Lakes Region (Wis.)--Biography--Anecdotes. 6. Middle West--Social life and customs--20th century--Anecdotes. 7. Farm life--Middle West--Anecdotes. 8. Material culture--Middle West--Anecdotes. I. Apps, Jerold W., 1934- Symbols. II. Title.
    F587.W3A555 2005
    977.5'043--dc22

                              2005004847

Dedication

For Ruth

Acknowledgments

Writing a book requires help from many. Elmer Marting of Monona, Iowa, contacted several people in Iowa for me to interview and traveled with my photographer son and me as we gathered Iowa material. Dr. Daryl Watson, Executive Director of the Galena-Jo Daviess County Historical Society and Museum, shared rural history of northwestern Illinois and introduced me to several people in his county. Dick Paisley, longtime rural mail carrier in Holy Cross, Iowa, spun story after story about his days delivering mail. Mike Brietbach, owner of Brietbach's tavern in Balltown, Iowa, shared family stories—and introduced us to his tavern's great meals and outstanding pie.

Walter Bjoraker, Professor Emeritus at the University of Wisconsin-Madison and a Minnesota farm boy, shared wonderful stories of his growing-up years.

Bernard Zelenske, longtime Redgranite, Wisconsin, barber, helped me understand what a small-town barbershop was like from Depression days to the present. My brother, Don Apps, a barber and former barbershop owner, added his stories to the mix of barber tales and read the material to make sure I portrayed the barber business correctly (mostly).

Laverne Forest deserves special mention. Not only did he allow me to interview him at length, but he harnessed up his team and allowed photos to be taken.

Bob Williams, Coordinator of Fairs, Wisconsin Department of Agriculture, Trade and Consumer Protection, shared the history of fairs and their importance to rural communities.

Dr. Jim Leary, Director of the Folklore Program at the University of Wisconsin-Madison, shared his vast knowledge of polka bands, card playing, and country taverns in the upper Midwest.

My son, Steve Apps, staff photographer at the *Wisconsin State Journal* in Madison, took all the photographs for this book, often under rather trying conditions. Many times we traveled together; he photographed while I interviewed. I've finally learned to stick to interviewing and let him decide which photos are best.

My wife, Ruth, read every word of this book, some sections several times. Without her help, this work would be nearly impossible. My daughter, Sue, in Columbus, Ohio, and my son, Jeff, in Colorado, also read and commented on several parts of the book.

And finally, to all the folks at Amherst Press, especially Roberta and Chuck Spanbauer, my continuing thanks for support and encouragement.

Contents

Symbols

They are all around us and we take them for granted. They are the symbols of our rural past, scattered throughout the countryside, on farmsteads, in villages, and at the crossroads where dusty trails once converged. Many are easily seen, others less so as time has aged, rusted, and hidden them behind the icons of progress.

These symbols are reminders of early home life in the country, work on the farm, how rural people kept in touch, the importance of community, and how farm folks relaxed and had fun.

Some of the symbols have little or no practical use today: windmills, threshing machines, water-driven grist mills, walking plows. Others are as significant now as they were a hundred years ago: country churches, rural mail carriers, telephones, and polka bands.

All the symbols are important, whether practical or not, for they are reminders of our histories, of the days when our ancestors worked the land, raised their children, shared with their neighbors, and passed on a legacy of values and beliefs to future generations.

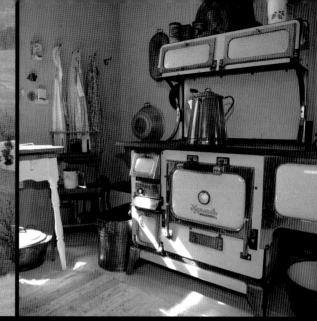

Lamps and Lanterns

Lamps and lanterns are reminders of those days before electricity—a time when farmers worked by the dim light of a lantern. Their children did homework at the kitchen table crowded up to an Aladdin lamp if they were fortunate or by the yellow glow of a glass lamp. Their mothers often mended socks, repaired overalls, cooked, baked, and did all the household chores with the poor light of a kerosene lamp. Some look back at those days with nostalgia; others remember never being able to see well after the sun went down.

A kerosene lamp sits on the kitchen table before dawn, casting a yellow light throughout the bone-chilling room. The freshly started fire in the kitchen stove snaps and pops and sends up the occasional thread of thin, gray smoke from the cracks around the stove lids. I pick up my barn lantern from its place near the wood box, lift the glass globe with a small lever provided for that purpose, take a match from the matchbox hanging on the wall near the stove, strike it and touch the flame to the wick. I close the globe, and another soft light competes with the one cast by the glass lamp on the table.

I head out to the barn for the morning milking. The lantern creates long shadows on the snow, strange, eerie, sometimes scary shadows for a ten-year-old. I often wonder what is out there, beyond the dim yellow lantern light in the shadows of the predawn morning.

In the barn, I hang my lantern on a nail in the ceiling back of the cows. Pa's lantern already hangs from another nail at the other end of the barn. I mumble, "Good morning," grab up a milk pail and stool, slide under a cow, and begin milking. Between the cows where we milk is near darkness, not unpleasant, for I can doze while milking and Pa can't notice. Sitting under a cow is clearly the warmest place on the farm this frigid morning, and hand milking doesn't require much light.

With the milking finished, I slip the wire handle of the lantern over my arm, and go hand over hand up the ladder to the barn's haymow. I find the nail to hang the lantern, a spot selected where forked hay is least likely to hit the lantern and cause a fire.

Long threads of frost-covered cobwebs hang from the beams of the barn. Lantern light reflects from the frosty cobwebs, making the scene beautiful and eerie at the same time. With a little imagination, I make out giant bears with squinty eyes and sharp teeth; I see mammoth birds not known to this part of the world, swooping down on me, snatching me up and hauling me away. I squelch my imagination and begin forking frost-covered hay, alfalfa and timothy, down the hay chutes to the hungry cattle below.

With the cows milked and fed, I take my lantern to the house, blow it out and set it in the corner of the kitchen. I will repeat the morning ritual again in the early evening and every day throughout the long Midwestern winter.

History of Lamps and Lanterns

Lamps were intended for indoor use, lanterns for outdoor lighting. In the early 1800s, lanterns were wooden or metal boxes with a candle inside. Whale oil became available, and lamps with wicks began appearing in the 1820s. By the 1830s, glass had improved, and glass globes began appearing on lamps and lanterns.

The popularity of lamps and lanterns increased rapidly after Canadian geologist Abraham Gesner, in 1849, patented a process to refine liquid fuel from coal. Gesner named this fuel kerosene after keros, which means wax. It had properties similar to paraffin oils. By 1857, refiners began deriving kerosene from petroleum, a process easier than taking it from coal.

By the late 1850s, kerosene was available in grocery and hardware stores, and by the 1890s could be ordered from Sears, Roebuck and Company.

With improved glass globes and with kerosene readily available, the switch from candles to lamps took place quickly. From 1874 to 1884 the use of kerosene for lighting increased from 1.5 gallons per person per year to 3.6 gallons. It cost about eight cents a gallon.

Lamp and lantern manufacturers flourished during the late 1800s and into the early 1900s. Many kinds of lamps became available, from those attached to the wall to a revolutionary new lighting device, the Aladdin lamp. Victor Samuel Johnson introduced the Aladdin lamp in 1909. He took the name Aladdin from the story of Aladdin and his lamp. It had a round wick, and the flame heated a mantle, causing it to glow and give light. An advertisement for the Aladdin lamp boasted: "The necessity of huddling around the table or burning several lamps in the same room no longer exists in the Aladdin-lighted home…. It lights up every part of the room."

A kerosene lamp, depending on the cleanliness of its glass globe, the trim of its wick, and the height of its flame, gave off light equivalent of five to 14 candles. By the turn of the century, some lamp makers claimed that their lamps equaled the light of 33 or more candles.

Along with improvements in lamps, lanterns were also improving. Manufacturers attached wire guards to protect the lantern's glass globes starting in the 1850s. The wire guards made them sturdier and safer for use in farm buildings such as chicken houses, cow and horse barns. By the 1850s, manufacturers mass-produced lanterns and sold them throughout the country. Dietz & Company of New York City, became a leading lantern maker and held onto its leadership for the next 25 years. The light of Dietz lanterns was the equivalent of ten to 12 candles.

Farmsteads

The history of the Midwest is written in the farmsteads scattered throughout the region, in the houses and grand old barns, in the silos and outhouses, the smokehouses and well houses, the summer kitchens and windmills.

Viewing farmsteads is the main reason that many urban people enjoy traveling in the countryside. Beyond their aesthetic appeal, farmsteads symbolize the history of the region. Each farm building has a story to tell of farming from settlement days, when the land was broken with oxen, to today, when mammoth tractors roar up and down the fields and family farms are disappearing.

I always knew when a city salesman arrived at our farm. He was usually trying to sell some fancy cattle or hog feed to Pa. Driving into a farmyard was like driving into a small village and seeing buildings all around you. On our farmstead the buildings were arranged around an area we called the dooryard. To the north was the farmhouse with attached woodshed, west of the house the chicken house, and then to the south a machine shed and granary. A little farther south was a combination wagon shed with corncribs on either side, then the barn and the silo, and to the east, the pump house. What the salesmen couldn't see was a brooder house in the southwest corner of the farmstead, another machine shed behind the granary, and the outhouse, tucked under a pine tree north of the house.

If the salesman arrived while I was doing chores in the chicken house, granary, or barn, I watched as he gingerly stepped from his car, said some kind words to our farm dog Fanny, and looked all around. Usually he would head for the house, and that's when I found out if the salesman knew anything about farmsteads. If he walked to the front door, I immediately branded him "city" because no farmer ever used the front door. Front doors were for show and often couldn't even be opened.

Sometimes I would make myself known and ask if I could help. But other times, depending on how the guy was dressed, what kind of fancy car he drove, and what Fanny thought of him by how much she barked, I let him stew in his ignorance.

History of Farmsteads

Studying farmsteads is a way to follow changes in agriculture, says Daryl Watson, Executive Director of the Galena-Jo Daviess County Historical Society and Museum in Galena, Illinois. "The earliest farmsteads were simple affairs," he said. "They were located on the south or east flank of the hills so the strong winds wouldn't hit them. If possible, they were located near a spring so the farmer didn't have to haul water for his livestock."

According to the 1855 Census of Illinois Agriculture, the average Illinois farmer had three or four cows, a half-dozen pigs, a few sheep, some oxen, and two horses or mules—mules were often preferred. The farmstead consisted of a barn and house, a corncrib, granary, and some smaller structures. Many of the early barns were log.

Both English and German people settled in northwestern Illinois, and they had different priorities for constructing their farmsteads. "For the Germans," Watson said, "the money went first into the barn; the house came second. For the English, about the same amount of money went into the house and barn, or maybe some of the English would pay more attention to the house."

Walter Bjoraker, Professor Emeritus, University of Wisconsin-Madison, remembers the Minnesota farmstead where he grew up. He was born in 1920, one of 13 children, on a farm about ten miles south and a little east of Owatonna. Bjoraker's father had come to the United States from Norway in 1882, at the age of 18.

The Bjoraker farmstead consisted of a farmhouse with a nearby summer kitchen and woodshed and the always-present outhouse. The barns included a cow barn with room for 15 cows and a horse barn with seven horse stalls. The horse barn was built in 1906 and the cow barn in 1908.

A buggy shed, which later became a blacksmith shop and workshop, stood near the barn. The milk house, located between the house and the barns, housed a well and a windmill-operated pump.

The Bjorakers smoked hams and dried beef in a small slant-roofed smokehouse attached to the milk house. When the smoking was completed, they took the hams, sides of bacon and dried beef; put them in flour sacks, and buried the meat in the oat bin in the granary until needed.

The Bjoraker farmstead also included a two-part chicken house for a hundred Rhode Island Red laying hens and a brooder house where setting hens hatched chicks.

As farming changed in the Midwest, so did farmsteads. Grand old dairy barns disappeared as farmers left behind dairy farming and moved to growing corn, soybeans, and other cash crops. In some instances, dairy barns were replaced with long, sprawling, single-story, open-sided barns. In the corn and soybean regions of the Midwest, older farmsteads were torn down as farms became larger and the number of farmers less.

Silos

Silos are silent sentinels on the rural horizon, exclamation points standing beside red barns. Silos are reminders of the days when farmers looked for a winter feed and stumbled onto something revolutionary—silage, a fermented feed, different from hay and dry grain but relished by livestock.

The silo on our home farm was nothing special. It was wooden, about thirty feet tall, eight feet across, and painted red, like the barn. When I was twelve, I learned an important lesson because of that silo. Every September, after the corn had developed ears but the plant was still green, we filled the silo. In a fashion somewhat like threshing, neighbors came by to help haul the recently cut corn to the silo filler, which chopped the corn plants (ears, stalks, and leaves) into little pieces and blew them up a long metal pipe through a window at the top of the structure.

Ross Caves, who was the local cattle trucker, owned a silo filler and hired out to farmers in our neighborhood. The afternoon before we were to fill, he arrived on our farm to set up the machine He bolted together the proper number of metal filler pipes while they lay on the ground. Then he leaned a long wooden extension ladder against the silo and instructed whoever was handy to crawl up the ladder with a rope and feed it through a pulley so the pipes could be pulled into place.

He pointed to me. I grabbed the rope and started up the ladder, hand after hand, looking upward as I climbed. I felt good. This job was something new and I could do it. I was an important contributor to the silo-filling operation. When I got to the top of the silo, near the little window, I fed the end of the rope through the pulley. But at this point I made a terrible mistake: I looked down. A wave of horror throbbed through me, and I wrapped both arms around the top rung of the ladder as tight as I could. I could feel sweat bubbling on my forehead, and I didn't move. Couldn't move.

"You all right, Jerry?" Ross called.

"Yup," I answered feebly. But I wasn't all right. I was terrified. I was certain this was it, that death was staring me in the face.

Ross Caves had obviously seen this condition before. He began climbing the ladder, talking to me gently about how I should step down a rung, move one of my hands while keeping hold with the other. After what seemed a very long time, I was on the ground, white and shaking. Ross said he wouldn't tell anyone what had happened. I learned a difficult lesson that day. I was afraid of heights. I still am.

History of Silos

Some claim that the first silo was built in McHenry County, Illinois, in 1873. It was horizontal, ten feet wide, 16 feet long, and 24 feet high with eight feet underground.

Others say a German immigrant farmer built the first silo in the United States in 1865, in Troy, New York. For years many farmers considered silos to be novelties and even problems. Some cheese factories refused to accept milk from farmers who fed their cows silage. Even the farm press had trouble accepting silos. One farm editor wrote, "Practical farmers won't adopt it, except here and there, and in ten years from now the silos being built will be used for storing potatoes, turnips, beets or ice."

Slowly silos caught on, thanks to the work of innovative farmers who were unafraid to take a chance, and to researchers such as F. H. King at the University of Wisconsin-Madison who introduced a wooden, cylindrical silo in 1891. Earlier upright silos had been rectangular, and silage spoiled in the corners. By the 1920s, silos were accepted, and they began appearing on dairy and livestock farms throughout the country.

Most early silos were wooden, although some upright models were of fieldstone construction. Silos were also constructed of poured concrete, brick, concrete stave, tile, concrete blocks, and metal. In the late 1940s the A. O. Smith Company of Milwaukee began making blue metal silos (Harvestores), which became quite popular.

Silage continues as a major feed source for dairy cattle, but many of today's silos are bunkers, horizontal structures with concrete bottoms and sides, and no tops. Also popular are tube silos consisting of white plastic tubes about four feet in diameter that are full of cut corn or hay and look like giant grub worms behind the barn.

Weather Vanes

The old weather vanes, some only a few inches tall, some several feet, are reminders of a time before TV weather maps and continuous weather channel forecasts, a time when farmers depended on knowing wind direction for predicting the weather and planning the coming day's activities.

On our farm, weather vanes had a major purpose beyond showing wind direction. Our weather vane was a target, a wonderful challenge for my BB gun, and a reason for competitive shooting when a neighbor boy came by toting his gun.

Shooting the weather vane with a BB gun seldom evoked much comment from Pa; but if he ever caught one of us shooting at it with a .22 rifle, there was trouble. A .22 rifle bullet made a hole in a weather vane that someone could easily spot from the ground.

On a late fall Saturday afternoon, Pa and Ma had gone to town, and my brothers and I were home alone.

I doubt anything would have happened except the Kolka boys stopped by for a visit. Jim and Dave were the ages of my brothers and me, and they had brought along a .22 rifle.

We got to talking, as kids will, about who was the best shot. Soon the boasts got to claims of lighting kitchen matches at fifty feet and splitting a bullet on a knife blade stuck in a block of wood.

Then Jim said he figured he could hit the weather vane on the barn while standing under the elm tree by the house—a considerable distance. He said he bet I couldn't. So we stood elbow to elbow with our .22s, aiming at the weather vane. My brothers were counting. When they got to three, we were to shoot. I don't remember whether we talked about how we would know who had hit the metal cow when we both shot at the same time. Discussing details like this sometimes spoiled an otherwise superior competitive event.

At the count of three, we both shot. The weather vane spun around two or three times.

"I hit it!" Jim yelled.

"I'm the one who hit it!" I yelled back.

We could spot only one additional hole in the weather vane, beyond the one that had been there for years. We declared the shooting a tie, each of us claiming victory.

A few days later, Pa asked if I knew whether anybody had shot at the weather vane.

"Why do you ask?" I said innocently.

"It's got two holes and it only had one."

I hadn't realized that Pa kept such close tabs on something as mundane as a weather vane. From that day forward, we chose other targets for our competitive shooting events.

History of Weather Vanes

Beyond showing wind direction, helping predict weather, and providing a target for farm kids, a weather vane was an attractive decoration on an otherwise rather dull expanse of barn roof. A weather vane usually included an arrow to catch the wind and letters indicating the four directions. These were the simplest; many were more complicated. Some consisted of flat metal replicas of farm animals. In dairy country, cows were common, old-fashioned cows with horns. Other weather vanes were roosters, pigs, eagles, or deer—sometimes even fish and whales and Model-T Ford cars.

In the Midwest, most of the big cow barns built just before and after the start of the 20th century had weather vanes. They were often perched on cupolas, the little building-like structures on the top of barn roofs. Lightning rods were often a part of weather vanes, with the lightning rod spike reaching toward the heavens. Many of the old weather vanes remain; each connected to its own set of stories.

Outhouses

Although few remain today, outhouses are reminders of a time before people had running water and indoor plumbing. Each farm and most village homes had one; few people talked about them, except city visitors who turned up their noses and declared them the worst part of country living, especially in winter.

I'd never thought much about an outhouse until I started country school. Of course at home, we had an outhouse tucked under a tree a short hike from the backdoor of the house. I visited it regularly but saw nothing special about the building. I seldom dawdled there, except on warm summer days, when I might page through the ever-present Sears catalog, glancing at hunting equipment and sneaking a peak at pictures of women's underwear. Most of the time the visit was to take care of business and be on my way.

When I started going to school, my perspective on outhouses changed. At Chain O' Lake School, where I attended for eight years, we had two outhouses located at opposite corners of the schoolyard. The girls' was in the northwest corner of the grounds, the boys' in the southwest corner.

At first, these outhouses seemed no different from the one we had at home. The size was the same, the equipment was the same—I say that without really knowing what was inside the girls' outhouse—and the smells were no different. But soon I discovered that the school outhouses had characteristics that went far beyond those of the humble structure at the end of the path behind our farmhouse.

About the third day of school, I noticed that a group of older boys had gathered behind the boys' toilet during recess and at noon, too, when we weren't otherwise playing softball, "Run Sheep Run," "Annie-I-Over," or other school games.

I asked George Jeffers what they were doing.

"You're too little to know," he answered.

"I am not," I replied.

"Got to be in third grade," George replied smugly.

Now my curiosity had peaked. I needed to know what was going on during these exclusive meetings behind the boys' toilet. I tried various ways of finding out. Most obvious was to keep asking the boys I saw there what they were doing. All I got was smiles and "You'll find out soon enough."

Sometimes I would stand around, pretending to do something important like drawing a picture in the sand with a stick while I tried to overhear what happened. On occasion I'd pick up a swearword or two and hear some loud laughter, but that was about all.

By the time I finally got to third grade, I had it mostly figured out. Behind the boys' toilet is where you learned the most up-to-date cuss words, what sex was all about, and what dirty tricks to pull on the teacher without getting caught.

I was right. At my initiation meeting, the older boys gathered around me and began their instruction with, "Don't you tell a soul, not your brothers, not your Pa, not a neighbor, and especially not the teacher what we do here."

"I won't," I replied, my eyes wide with excitement.

They then took turns rattling off cuss words that they thought I didn't know. I acted like I didn't, but I'd been hearing these words for years. The sex information was more interesting, especially when it got down to comparing what went on in the barnyard with what happened in bedrooms. This was good stuff, even though I had to listen to a batch of cuss words I already knew before we got to it. As the years passed, I completely changed my attitude toward outhouses, especially those in country schoolyards. The education behind the boys' toilet came mighty close to being as interesting as the lessons inside the schoolhouse; some days it was far more interesting.

History of Outhouses

People called outhouses outdoor toilets, biffies, backhouses, privies, rest rooms, facilities, comfort stations, necessaries, relief stations, latrines (a military term), heads (for navy people), and bathrooms, although no one ever took a bath in one.

Most rural outhouses had a floor, four sides and a roof, plus a seat-like bench with two holes—thus the language "two-holer." Inside, pictures were often nailed to the wall; photos cut from magazines or calendars were popular. On the outhouse seat was the ever-present Sears catalog, last year's model being recycled.

Outside of the smell, which was controlled to some extent by tossing lime down the holes, a visit to the outhouse in summer was a rather pleasant experience. Outhouses were usually in the shade, they were reasonably well ventilated, and they offered a chance to listen to birds and commune with nature.

Visiting the little building in winter could be a dreadful experience. After a run through deep snow, the visitor might find a snowdrift in front of the door that had to be kicked aside before he could enter. The seat soaked up the chill and always felt many degrees colder than the outside temperature. Visits were brief. Even to a country person, visiting an outhouse in winter had elements of humor. Not often did someone have most of his body covered with heavy shirts and coats while one part was completely bare.

Outhouse lore is best known at Halloween. Traditionally, outhouses were targets of Halloween pranksters. It didn't matter whether the outhouse was in back of a church, a country school, or a farm home; many were tipped over at Halloween. The stories of such occurrences are many, often involving the fact that someone was in the outhouse when it was flipped, and he couldn't get out because the outhouse lay on its door. It is bathroom humor at its worst, to envision someone caught in an overturned outhouse in the middle of the night, his head thrust through one of the holes, and the sound of an embarrassed..."Help!" coming from the structure.

Outhouses remain, especially on farmsteads. They stand alone, forgotten it seems, but the memories of them and their stories continue.

Clotheslines

Clotheslines recall memories of bedsheets smelling as fresh as the summer wind and shirts, pants, socks, and underwear feeling as soft and fluffy as puppy fur.

A clothesline with freshly washed clothes flapping in the breeze is a reminder of the days before automatic washing machines and dryers with their bevy of buttons and dials that can be set to match the fabric being washed or dried.

On washday, before electricity and running water came to our farm, my brothers and I carried countless pails of water from the pump house to the kitchen, enough to fill the copper boiler sitting on the wood stove. In the early days, the windmill pumped the water. On a calm day we dipped water from the stock tank. Later, a gasoline engine did the pumping. It was dependable but slow.

While my brothers and I were carrying water, Pa dragged the Speed Queen washing machine, powered by a Briggs & Stratton gasoline engine, from the woodshed into the kitchen. He stuck the exhaust pipe outside through a crack in the door. Some days the washing machine motor started on the third or fourth push—he kicked a foot-operated lever while he pulled on the choke wire. Pa usually didn't choke it enough, or he choked it too much, for the machine sat there refusing to come to life. The water in the copper boiler was steaming, as was Pa, as he stomped on the kick lever again and again. Finally, after a half-hour or so, the machine made a feeble "pop," which was the encouragement Pa needed to go on. Soon we heard a couple of pops, then a series of pops, and finally continuous pops, and washday began. The washing machine had its own ringer to squeeze out the excess sudsy water before the clothes tumbled into the rinse water tub, where Ma swished them around before pushing them through the ringer again.

When the clothes were washed, my brothers and I carried out the dirty wash water and dumped it beyond the ash pile in the backyard.

Unless the temperature was below zero, Ma hung the clothes on the clothesline that ran from near the house to almost as far as the outhouse. Before hanging the clothes, she always ran a cloth along each wire line to remove any rust that may have accumulated since the last washday.

A clothesline filled with newly washed clothes was quite a sight: white sheets blowing in the breeze, rows of socks, long underwear swinging legs and arms, and Ma's "unmentionables" carefully hung on the line so that sheets and shirts would shield them from any gawking passerby.

On cold days the clothing froze stiff. Ma brought the frozen clothes into the kitchen to thaw. She leaned the bib overalls and long johns against the kitchen wall; they looked like men who had come to visit, all lined up in a row, as if waiting for a meal. As these frozen mannequins thawed, they slowly crumpled to the floor.

I will always remember the expression on Ma's face when the Monday washing was done and all the clothes were hung on the clothesline. It was the same look of satisfaction that Pa had when we finished shocking a field of oats or digging a patch of potatoes. It was a rural person's quiet reward for hard work and a job completed.

History of Clotheslines

Clotheslines were located close to the farmhouse and often along the path to the outhouse. The lines, six or more, were usually strung between two cedar posts deeply set in the ground so that there would be no "give" to the lines when they were loaded with wet clothes. A two-by-four to which the lines were attached was bolted near the top of each post. The composition of the lines varied considerably. At one time, clothesline wire was the same kind used to repair fences. It was strong and durable; but it rusted, and that rust transferred to the clothes.

Store-bought clothesline was better. It usually had a metal core covered with fabric—tough and rustproof. Clotheslines were strung about chin high, not so high that they couldn't be easily reached, not so low that the clothing dragged on the ground. Sometimes clothesline height proved a problem.

A story is told about the hired man who found it necessary to run for the outhouse one Monday morning. Somehow he failed to see the clothesline that hit him just under the chin, upending him.

"I'm so sorry," said the farmer's wife, who was hanging up clothes nearby.

"It's okay. I wouldn't have made it anyway," answered the embarrassed hired man.

Modern day clotheslines often consist of a single metal pole stuck in the ground, with lines that can be folded against the pole when not in use. Or more often, a clothesline might be a single line running from a farm building to a post, nothing like the clotheslines of earlier days.

Woodpiles

Woodpiles are reminders of life before central heating and oil- and gas-fired furnaces. For those growing up in the country, woodpiles elicit memories of hard work, when "making wood" was as important as making hay or threshing grain. Those who recall those woodpile days remember the many times they were warmed as they cut and split wood, and the pride felt when they had constructed a beautiful woodpile.

In my neighborhood a big woodpile made a statement to those driving by. A substantial woodpile said of a farmer, "I'm ready for the worst kind of winter." Woodpiles also demonstrated neatness and attention to detail—important values for any rural person, but especially important for farmers. Pa would often say, "Just look at Severson's nice woodpile." A translation of *nice* revealed first that Severson had a big woodpile, not some little dump of wood sticks but a pile of blocks as high as the tallest man in the neighborhood and as long as the chicken house. A second meaning of *nice* was the way the split blocks were piled on top of each other, end to end with the split sides showing, forming a roof.

Severson's woodpile was the kind that people noticed and talked about; it made them stand out among the neighbors and gave them a place of prominence. Severson's woodpile also evoked envious comment from those with lesser woodpiles. "If Severson spent as much time with his cows as he did with his woodpile, maybe his cows would amount to something, too." Or, "Jeez, Severson and his wife must have cold blood. They need all that wood to keep warm? You'd think they lived in Alaska."

Although neighbors commented about the size and beauty of woodpiles and what made a *nice* woodpile, nobody acknowledged that a woodpile was temporary. It was put up to be taken down. The colder the winter, the faster a woodpile disappeared.

A popular myth associated with woodpiles and burning wood is, "He who saws his own wood is twice warmed." This is a lie, a real whopper of a mistruth. First, let's correct the language. No rural person ever talked about *sawing* his own wood. You "made wood." During the process of making wood, you did some sawing, but there were many other opportunities for warming beyond sawing.

To start, you hiked out to the woods—no rural person ever said, "I'm going to the forest." Nothing would brand you a city guy faster than talking about forests and going out into them. Forests were somewhere else, maybe in Colorado or Oregon. But not in the Midwest. In the Midwest, there were woods, lots of woods.

After you had hiked into the woods in search of trees to cut, you had already warmed yourself once, even before you found a suitable tree. Suitable trees were those that had recently died—the wood would take less time to dry than wood from live trees. First, you notched the tree with an ax on the side of the tree toward which you hoped it would fall. Depending on how cold it was, you could work up a terrific sweat notching a tree. You'd probably sweat more as you and a partner pulled a crosscut saw back and forth as many times as it took to fell the tree.

When the tree began tipping, you yelled "Timber!" and rushed out of the way because a cut tree often defied even the most skilled notcher and sometimes fell in a different direction than planned. The terror of running from a giant oak tree falling toward you was yet another way to get warm.

With the tree on the ground, next came trimming off the smaller branches with an ax and sawing the larger limbs and the trunk so that they could be hoisted onto a horse-drawn, steel-wheeled wagon or onto a bobsled if it was winter.

With the wood toted to the farmstead, the wood-sawing bee came next, a day when the neighbors helped. A huge engine-driven circle saw was shoved into place, and the logs and limbs were sliced into blocks; a major opportunity for personal warming. Now came splitting, knocking the blocks apart with wedges and mauls so the wood fit into the several wood stoves on the farm.

There were yet two more opportunities for warming:

carrying the wood from the woodpile to the woodshed and lugging the wood from the woodshed to the wood boxes beside the kitchen stove, the dining room stove, the pump house stove, and the wood stove in the potato cellar that kept the potato harvest from freezing.

History of Woodpiles

Nearly every Midwestern farm had a woods, sometimes more than one. A woods ranged from a few acres—three or four, to quite a few—30 or 40.

Hilly farms had more woods than flat farms. Usually the hilliest part of a farm was left as woods. The trees commonly found in a Midwestern woods were oak (white, red, black, and burr), pine (white, red, Scotch, and jack), aspen, birch, cedar, maple, hickory, walnut, cherry, and poplar, depending on how far north was the woodlot, what kind of soil it was, and how much moisture was available.

Rural people knew their trees and which ones made the best firewood. Oaks, hickory, walnut, cherry, and maple provided the most lasting heat. Aspen, pine, and cedar were good woods for starting a fire and providing enough heat to cook a pot of coffee or fry a skillet of eggs and bacon.

Kitchen Stoves

A kitchen stove, cussed when ashes spilled on the floor or smoke billowed up from around the lids, was often taken for granted in farm kitchens. It served quietly, day after day, requiring little care but contributing much to farm family life. Seeing one today is a reminder that the kitchen stove was once the hub of all activity in the farm kitchen and in winter, the center of all activity in the house.

It was a cold, windy winter day with light snow sifting across the open area between our house and barn. A day to stay inside after the chores, crowd close to the kitchen stove, smell fresh bread baking in the oven, and catch the occasional whiff of oak smoke puffing up from around the stove lids when the wind gusted.

A knock on the door.

"Come on in," said Pa, without getting up from his chair.

"Wonder who it is?" Ma said.

"Clem, what're you doin' walkin' around on a day like this?" was Pa's way of greeting Clem Radloff, who lived about a mile north of our farm and who often walked over for a visit.

"Needed some fresh air," Clem replied. He brushed snow from his red plaid Mackinaw coat and shook the snow from his black cap with its cat-fur earflaps.

"Good day to sit by the fire," Pa said, motioning Clem to a chair beside the stove. Clem Radloff was short, about five feet five or so, and rather thin. His usually red face was even redder today.

"Dang sight colder than I thought," Clem said, blowing

on his hands as he rubbed them together over the stove.

Soon Clem was sitting in a chair, drinking black coffee and eating a sugar cookie that Ma had retrieved from the cookie jar.

"Some kind of winter, we're havin'," Pa offered.

"Yup," Clem answered.

"Can't remember it being this cold, this long."

"Nope," said Clem.

And so the conversation continued the entire afternoon, with many *yups* and *nopes*, and little information exchanged.

"Gotta be going," Clem finally said. "Like to get home before dark."

"Good of you to stop by," Pa said.

"Yup," answered Clem. Then he added, "Oh, by the way, suppose you could come over on Saturday? I wanna saw some wood. Bring Jerry along."

"Sure, we'll be there."

And thus we learned the reason for Clem's visit, as he went out the door. When neighbors gather around the kitchen stove, getting to the reason for the visit takes awhile—and sometimes there is no reason.

History of Kitchen Stoves

Thousands of cast-iron kitchen stoves were manufactured in the late 1800s and early 1900s. They were placed at one end of the farm kitchen near an outlet to the chimney. A black stovepipe with a damper to control draft led from the chimney outlet to the back of the stove. Once a year, in the springtime usually, the stovepipe was taken down, carried out to the ash pile located at the back of the house, and pounded to remove the year's worth of accumulated soot. Different from the other wood stoves located on the farmstead, the kitchen stove was in service all year, not just during the winter months.

Kitchen stoves were massive hulks of iron, decorated here and there with silver scrolling that forever needed cleaning. The warming oven was above the stove. The oven was an enclosed compartment with two doors facing front, located on either side of the stovepipe and protruding over the stove top far enough to capture some heat. The cook put bread dough in the warming oven to rise and stashed pies there to keep them warm. This was also a good place to dry wet mittens. The stove top usually consisted of six removable cast-iron stove lids. The two lids farthest to the left were directly over the firebox and provided the hottest heat. Farther to the right, less heat was available. The cook knew all this and moved the cooking pots, skillets, teakettles, and coffeepots depending on whether high heat or mere warming was required.

On ironing day, sadirons replaced the cooking pots and the wood of choice was oak, which provided an even, long-lasting heat to keep the sadirons at a constant temperature. If the farm wife wasn't cooking or ironing, but wanted the stove to heat the kitchen well into the night, the choice might be white oak or maple.

The stove's reservoir was located to the far right of the cooking area, alongside the oven. The covered reservoir was the family's source of warm water for washing and other warm water needs. The oven door, often open on cold days to allow the oven heat to permeate through the room, was a place where farmers propped their feet to warm them. The oven itself, with no temperature controls except for the amount and kind of wood put in the firebox, turned out wonderful pies, cakes, cookies, beef roasts, casseroles and, of course, countless loaves of homemade bread.

The ash drawer was under the firebox; it was a daily task to pull it out and carry the ashes to the ash pile in the backyard.

Behind the kitchen stove a farmer warmed baby pigs born too early in the spring, nurtured newly arrived baby chicks, and placed an old coat for the farm dog to sleep on during cold winter nights.

During the cold months, everyone in the family bathed in front of the wood stove (on Saturday night), one at a time, in a galvanized washtub with hot water available from the stove's reservoir.

PART II: DOING THE WORK

Draft Horses

For more than 150 years, draft horses were the main source of power on farms; they plowed, planted, and harvested. They pulled high-wheeled wagons that hauled produce to market, and they dragged logs from the woods. In later years, they extracted Model-T Ford cars from muddy country roads. They were once as common on farms as tractors are today.

We had three horses on our home farm: Frank and Charlie, a pair of Percherons who were plodding and average but dependable, and Dick, a black mustang that someone said had come from a western ranch. Dick was stylish, he carried his head high and showed lots of spunk, but he wasn't dependable. Driving him was an adventure; you never knew what he would do and when he would do it. Pa usually drove him for those jobs when one horse was enough—cultivating potatoes or dragging logs out of the woods.

Frank and Charlie did the heavy work—plowing, disking, pulling the grain binder, hauling the hay wagon, snaking stones off the plowed cornfield. You asked Frank and Charlie to do a job and they did it, no matter how difficult. You asked Dick to do a job, and if he didn't want to tackle it, he might try to bite or kick you. You stayed awake when you worked with Dick.

For instance, we were butchering in early November on a cold, winter-like day. When the killing part was finished, Pa said he was going to fetch Dick and hitch him to the stone boat, a wooden sled used for toting stones from our fields. The stone boat would work well for hauling the dead pig to the shed where we had assembled the butchering equipment.

I saw Pa coming with Dick and the stone boat. Dick walked with his head high and his black tail swinging back and forth. He was truly a showy horse.

We lifted the pig's carcass onto the stone boat, and Pa clucked to Dick. They trotted off toward the shed and the butchering equipment. I walked along behind.

When the stone boat with the dead pig got about halfway to the shed, Dick must have caught a whiff of pig blood. He snorted a couple of times and threw his head into the air. Pa yelled, "Whoa!" but the command did nothing to quiet the black horse. He leaped into the air and bolted, yanking the reins from Pa's hands. Dick headed for the barn, for his stall where he always returned when things weren't going right for him. But the wooden barnyard gate was closed.

With one gigantic leap, Dick cleared the gate with feet to spare. Unfortunately, the stone boat with the dead pig didn't. They struck the wooden gate dead center. Boards and pieces of boards from the gate flew in every direction. The dead pig rolled off into the barnyard muck.

Dick, with what was left of the stone boat minus the dead pig, stood by the back door of the barn, his eyes rolling and his sides heaving. Pa soon had him under control, but Dick wanted nothing more to do with the stone boat and the dead pig. Pa hitched up Frank and Charlie, and they completed the task with scarcely a snort or a flick of their wiry tails.

History of Draft Horses

Although tractors became available by the 1920s, many farmers continued to work the land with horses. The most popular breeds were Belgians, Percherons, and Clydesdales. All had European roots: Belgians were obviously from Belgium, Percherons from France, and Clydesdales from Scotland.

Draft horses were multipurpose animals. In addition to the work they did on and off the farm, farm kids usually learned to ride a horse by climbing on the wide back of one of these dependable animals. For many farmers, their horses were like members of the family. Switching from horse power to tractor power was a difficult decision. Usually the horses stayed after the first tractor arrived. A farmer who had grown up with horses needed to have them around. They were a comfort during those years when tractors took over because horses always started on cold mornings.

Walking Plows

Walking plows are found in farm museums, tucked in the corners of farm sheds, and sometimes used to hold mailboxes. They are reminders of farming when farmers used horses to plow their fields, walking with one foot in the furrow and hoping the plow point would not hit a stone and leap out of the ground. Those old enough to recall horses and walking plows remember the first time their fathers asked them to plow with the team. It was clearly a rite of passage on the farm, a time when a boy became a man.

George Dietrich had recently moved into our neighborhood to take up farming. I remember the day he asked Pa to show him how to plow. Coming from Milwaukee, he had few farming skills. Somewhere he'd bought a used walking plow, and he had earlier purchased a team of horses.

When Pa and I arrived at Dietrich's place, he was hitching his team to the plow, a miserable implement unused for years. One of the wooden handles was wired together, and the moldboard, the part of the plow that turns the ground, was covered with rust.

"How do I get started?" Dietrich asked.

"Wait here," Pa said. He walked to the far end of the field where he tied a red handkerchief on a bush.

When Pa returned, he said, "Now we're ready to plow. See that handkerchief?"

"Yeah."

"Walk your team toward that handkerchief as straight as you can," Pa instructed.

The field Dietrich had selected for his plowing lesson was not an easy one. It was hilly and stony. Plowing with a walking plow was hard enough work when the ground was flat and there were no stones but was much tougher under hilly, stony conditions.

"Tie the harness lines together, George, and put them around your neck because you're gonna need both hands on the plow handles," Pa said.

With years of work in a Milwaukee factory, standing around watching some machine, Dietrich was about as strong as my eight-year-old brothers. His narrow shoulders weren't made for holding plow handles, either. He was a pitiful sight with the lines around his neck and his skinny arms trying to hold an unforgiving walking plow pulled by a rather worn-out and reluctant team.

"One more thing," Pa said before Dietrich began plowing. "Keep those plow handles out in front of you. You hit a stone when you're too close to the handles, and one will jump up and break a rib."

"Gid-up," said Dietrich. The team leaned into their harnesses, and the plow moved forward.

Before long I could see that Dietrich's arms were becoming tired because he was beginning to stand over the plow rather than letting it work out in front of him.

"Crack!" The plow unexpectedly struck a huge rock and jumped out of the ground; a plow handle caught Dietrich in the side. He fell to the ground. With the impact, the team stopped.

"You all right, George?" Pa asked after we ran to where George lay holding his side.

"I don't think so," said Dietrich. He was breathing in short gasps and holding his side.

"I told you to hold the plow out in front of you so this wouldn't happen,"

"But my arms got tired," Dietrich said.

We drove the team to the barn. Pa took Dietrich to the doctor, who discovered two broken ribs. Dietrich hired a man with a tractor plow to finish plowing his field.

History of Walking Plows

To support a crop, the ground had to be disturbed, and for thousands of years plowing was a way to do that. Early plows were wooden contrivances that dug a small trench in the ground when they worked well. More modern plows came when men learned to work with metals. Farmers in Colonial America plowed with cast-iron plows, which worked well in New England, but when pioneers moved West, richer Midwestern soils stuck to the plow bottoms. The problem became so serious that some settlers considered returning back East. At least in the East, their plows turned the soil without gumming up.

John Deere, born in Vermont in 1804, learned the blacksmith trade as a young man. Before 1830 Deere had established a reputation for quality work and inventiveness. He traveled West with the pioneers and in 1836 settled at Grand Detour, Illinois. There he built a forge and began making farm tools and implements. Deere heard about the plow problem and was convinced that if he polished a plow bottom, the heavy Midwestern soil wouldn't stick to it. He experimented with a steel plow made from a broken saw blade, and it workcd. Soon Deere was manufacturing plows from whatever pieces of steel he could find. To satisfy a great demand for this "self-polishing" plow, he imported steel from England. By 1847 John Deere was manufacturing one thousand plows a year.

Walking behind a plow was one of the toughest jobs on the farm; soon farmers were asking manufacturers to develop a riding plow. An early riding plow, called a sulky, could be purchased with either a 14- or 16-inch bottom (the size indicated the width of the furrow plowed). It had three wheels and a seat for the plowman. Sears, Roebuck offered a sulky plow for $24.75. Next came the "gang plow," a sulky plow with two plow bottoms. With these larger plows, three and often four horses were required to pull them. All horse-drawn plows were replaced when tractors came to the farm.

Windmills

Today, windmills stand like iron sentinels, sturdy yet fragile, and often taller than nearby barns and silos. Most of them are abandoned, resting after years of pumping water. Windmills also provided a ready target for farm boys and girls with BB guns who shot at the tail and listened for the ping of BBs striking steel. Farmers depended on them before gasoline engines and electric motors.

"Sure could use some rain," Pa said when I got to the barn for the morning milking. "This keeps up, the corn won't amount to anything. Cow pasture's mostly gone already."

It was August. It was hot and it was dry. Each morning the sun came up in a cloudless sky and shot the temperature into the nineties by noon. By late morning each day, a breeze began blowing, the windmill wheel began turning, and water flowed into the stock tank.

I milked my cows quietly, not knowing what to say. Everyone feared the damage that dry, hot weather brought on farm crops and farm animals.

"One good thing. Enough wind to keep the windmill pumping water. Don't know what we'll do if the wind quits," Pa said.

The next day the sun came up in a cloud of haze that hung on the horizon. No wind at midday, not even a hint of a breeze as the August sun cut through the dirty gloom.

"Got enough water for one more day," Pa said when we finished milking that evening and turned the cattle out to night pasture.

The stock tank was about half full, and we were

already pumping water by hand for Ma's use in the house. It was nearly impossible to pump enough water by hand for the cattle and horses. They could drink water faster than we could pump it.

The next day was a repeat of the previous one, if anything hotter. By noon the stock tank was empty. The cattle and horses gathered around it, trying to nudge each other out of the way for a drink of water. But there was no water. By suppertime the air was filled with the bellowing of thirsty cattle, an eerie, hopeless sound.

We milked the cows that evening, but they didn't want to be milked; they wanted to return to the stock tank. The bottom of the tank was as dry as the dust in the barnyard, and the bellowing for water continued through the night, keeping us from sleep.

The following morning, Pa called Allen Davis, our neighbor to the north, who pumped water with a gasoline engine. Allen agreed we could haul water from his pump. We loaded empty ten-gallon milk cans onto the wagon and headed for Allen's farm. For several hours we hauled water, enough to quiet the frantic bellowing and calm the cow herd.

By midafternoon, clouds built in the West, and by suppertime a breeze began blowing and the windmill started turning. Soon the stock tank was full.

"Gonna look into buyin' a gasoline engine," Pa said when we milked cows that night.

History of Windmills

Windmills have a long history. They ground flour and sawed wood, and in the lowlands of Europe they pumped water from one level to another. But for hundreds of years no one learned how to make a simple, inexpensive windmill that would pump well water. The early windmills were huge, clumsy machines made of masonry and wood with canvas sails—not something a farmer could use for pumping water.

In 1854 Daniel Halladay, a machinist, secured a patent for Halladay's Standard windmill, which would pump water. Meanwhile, Lawrence Wheeler experimented with a windmill that would turn out of the wind during a windstorm. A problem with early windmills was that they literally blew apart during storms. Wheeler patented his windmill in 1867 and with his son William began making the Wheeler Eclipse in Beloit, Wisconsin.

Through the 1870s, Halladay's Standard and Wheeler's Eclipse became the leading windmills manufactured in the United States. But because these windmills were of wooden construction—the blades were often made of cypress and the tower of oak—they were subject to weathering and rot.

The Matt Foos Company developed one of the first all-metal windmills in 1872. Thomas O. Perry conducted thousands of experiments on metal windmills, but his work was ignored because people knew that Halladay's Standard and Wheeler's Eclipse were quite dependable.

Perry met LaVerne Noyes, an inventor of farm implements, and in 1888 they began manufacturing an all-metal Aermotor windmill, described as "the first truly scientific windmill." In their first year of production, 24 Aermotors were sold. Four years later, 1892, the Aermotor Company sold 24,000 windmills. The machine was constructed of steel and cast iron. With earlier windmill models, the farmer had to climb the tower and grease the mechanism nearly every week. The Aermotor had enclosed gears and required greasing only twice yearly.

By the late 1800s, Aermotor had considerable competition. Well-known names included Dempster, Monitor, Challenge, and Fairbury (made of steel) and Monitor, Challenge, Dempster, Raymond, and Eclipse (made of wood).

Sears, Roebuck & Company offered both steel and wooden Kenwood windmills in their 1908 catalog. The steel windmills cost $13.75; the wooden windmills sold for $17.50. These prices did not include the towers. Sears sold towers starting at $12.92 for a 20-foot tower and as much as $63.70 for a 60-foot tower.

Windmill sales peaked in 1929. Soon after, many farmers replaced their water-pumping windmills with gasoline engines.

Gasoline Engines

From just before 1900 to the late 1940s, gasoline engines performed a variety of tasks that made farm life a little easier. They replaced wind, animal, and human power with mechanical power. Today they are seen at antique power shows, farm auctions, and occasionally tucked away in the corner of a farmer's shed. "Never can tell when I might need it," the farmer says.

I remember the day when the first gasoline engine arrived on our farm. A truck backed up to the pump house, and my father and the driver unloaded what appeared to be a huge hunk of cast iron. It was a Monitor gasoline engine with attached pump jack. (A pump jack consists of gears, pulleys, and two arms that lift and lower a pump rod, much like a windmill.)

After a couple hours of shifting and pushing, bolting and pounding, the engine and pump jack were in place. The engine stood about three feet tall, with a huge fly-wheel on one side and an open water-cooling tank on its top. A small tank for gasoline was fastened to one side of the engine—the first machine on our farm, besides our car, that required gasoline.

The truck driver said we should dump a cup of oil into the machine every week or so, to make sure the piston—which was about the size of two large men's fists put together—was lubricated. "And squirt a little oil on the moving parts every day, and it will serve you well."

He went on to demonstrate how to start the machine. "Here's what you do," he said. "Grab hold of this handle on the flywheel." He pointed to a wooden handle tucked into the huge cast-iron wheel. "Before you start turning, push on this little spring. It releases the pressure from the cylinder so it will turn easier. When the flywheel starts spinning, let go of the spring and it'll start."

I followed his directions, and with a bang and a shudder and a shake, the engine came to life. Because it was only one cylinder, it fired, then made all kinds of wheezing and puffing sounds before it fired again. Meanwhile, the cast-iron flywheel turned. The three of us stood watching, marveling at this wonderful machine.

"Let it warm up for a couple minutes, then push on

this lever and the pump jack will start."

Pa pushed the lever, the engine slowed some, the pops seemed louder and the vibrating a little more intense, but the pump jack began moving up and down. Soon water poured from the pump on its way to the water tank and the thirsty cows and horses.

Pa just stood there smiling, and I was probably grinning too because now we didn't have to depend on the wind. We could pump water when we wanted to, not when the wind allowed us to.

History of Gasoline Engines

Several inventors experimented with internal combustion engines in the late 1800s, as an alternative to steam engines that were simply too big and clumsy for most farmwork. The Fairbanks Morse Company, manufacturer of the Eclipse windmill, sold its first internal combustion engine in 1893 and soon was making gasoline-powered engines that ranged from 2$1/2$ to 65 horsepower.

The Fuller and Johnson Company of Madison, Wisconsin, advertised a "Farm Pump Engine," in the April 1911 *Farm Journal Magazine*. The ad read: "Fits any pump and makes it hump. Pumps 400 to 1,000 gallons per hour. No waiting for the wind. Fits any force pump and makes it go the limit. Supplies abundance of water, fresh from the well, for herds of stock."

Soon gasoline engines for pumping water were selling by the thousands. Farmers also used them for running milking machines, powering wood saws, and operating washing machines. Maytag, Speed Queen, and other washing machine manufacturers assembled their products with built-in gasoline engines.

Some farmers had gasoline-powered electrical systems—a gasoline engine, electrical generator, and banks of batteries. Most of these were 32-volt systems that allowed farmers to have electric lights and a few other electrical conveniences. Fairbanks Morse was one of the earliest to manufacture a home electricity-generating unit. Others makers of gasoline-powered electrical systems included Delco, Fuller and Johnson, Kohler, and GencoLight.

John Deere was also an early manufacturer of gasoline engines, and the Briggs & Stratton Corporation, with headquarters in Milwaukee, began making air-cooled gasoline engines in the early 1900s. Soon Briggs & Stratton engines were powering washing machines, concrete mixers, milking machines, portable saws, grain and hay elevators, and later, lawn mowers. By the late 1940s, Briggs & Stratton had become the largest manufacturer of small gasoline engines in the country.

When electricity arrived on the farm beginning in the late 1930s, gasoline engines slowly moved into storage.

Tractors

Tractors symbolize the shift from animal and human power to mechanical power. With a tractor, a farmer could work more acres in less time. Early farm tractors became the topic of conversation whenever farmers gathered. They debated which tractors were better: John Deere, Farmall, Allis-Chalmers, Ford. If the truth be known, many of these farmers would have preferred a good team of horses to any tractor.

In January of 1945, a truck rolled into our farmyard and stopped. The driver stepped out and walked to the house. I looked out the kitchen window and said that there was a truck in our yard and it was hauling a tractor and it must be lost.

Pa said the driver wasn't lost. In a few minutes a shiny red Farmall H tractor stood in our farmyard, a remarkable sight. Pa had often talked about the jobs a tractor could do that a team of horses couldn't, like pulling a two-bottom plow, running a threshing machine, and cultivating two rows of corn at once. Of course, horses could do

jobs that the Farmall couldn't, such as snaking logs out of the woods when the snow was belly deep and starting when it was thirty-below zero.

After the trucker left, Pa crawled on the seat, pushed on the starter button and the engine started. Soon he was driving around the farmyard, trying the different shifting gears, going at different speeds. I expected him to yell, "Whoa!" when he drove into the shed where the tractor was to be parked. But he didn't. One of our neighbors, Fred Jackson, got a new tractor a year earlier. His son told us that on the day he drove their new tractor into the shed, he started yelling "Whoa!" and was still yelling when the tractor smashed through the back of the shed and continued on up the hill and out into a field where the engine finally stalled. The tractor was scratched a little, but the main damage was to the shed. They had to replace an entire end. We all reminded Fred of this whenever we saw him. He just smiled and said nothing. He had

come to enjoy his new machine.

Even with our new tractor, Pa kept the horses for several more years and along the way added a Ford 8N and a Farmall C. The day eventually came when all our farmwork was done with tractors, and the horses were put out to pasture permanently.

History of Tractors

The first tractors on Midwestern farms were steam engines, which began appearing in the mid-1800s. Steam engines burned coal or wood and were huge, clumsy, smoke-spewing beasts on iron wheels. The J. I. Case Company of Racine, Wisconsin, began making steam engines in 1869 and by 1886 became the largest manufacturer of steam engines in the world.

By 1900 several inventors were experimenting with internal combustion engines. In 1892 John Froelich of Iowa, invented the first gasoline-powered tractor to go forward and backward. He later formed the Waterloo Gasoline Traction Engine Company located in Waterloo, Iowa.

The Hart-Parr Company (with beginnings in Madison, Wisconsin) developed a "gasoline traction engine" in 1902, after the company moved to Charles City, Iowa. It was a gasoline engine powered machine that could move itself. It weighed about 20,000 pounds and generated between 25 and 45 horsepower. In 1907 the Hart-Parr Company began calling their invention a "trac-tor."

In 1906 the International Harvester Company began manufacturing tractors. The early ones were called the Mogul and the Titan. Both were monster machines, primarily used for stationary work such as operating threshing machines. They consisted of a gasoline engine mounted on a steam engine chassis. The drive wheels were eight to ten feet in diameter and weighed as much as 20 tons. Other early manufacturers were Rumely, Hart-Parr, and International Harvester.

At first, farmers were skeptical of gasoline tractors. They could not comprehend that a machine could replace a horse, especially if they had grown up with horses and considered them partners in their farming operations.

Slowly, gasoline tractors became popular. In 1912 John Deere began experimenting with several kinds of tractors. By 1924 they were making the two-cylinder Model D. In 1907 Henry Ford developed what he called an "Automobile Plow," an experimental tractor made from automobile parts. Ford began manufacturing the Fordson tractor in 1917, and it became the first lightweight mass-produced tractor in the United States. By 1925 Ford had produced a half-million Fordson tractors. Later versions included the Ford 9N (1929) and the Ford 8N (1947). By 1950 several other tractor names appeared: Case, Ferguson, Allis-Chalmers, David Brown, Massey-Harris, Minneapolis-Moline, and Oliver. Tractors soon became as commonplace on farms as draft horses were before them.

Threshing Machines

Threshing machines are reminders of a time when farmers worked together to harvest their crops, to accomplish jobs they couldn't do alone. But there was more than hard work at these gatherings. They were also social events, a time for sharing and catching up on the news, for telling stories and, above all, for eating well.

When I was ten years old, my job was to shovel back oats in the grain bin. It was a tedious, backbreaking job, but I was a part of the threshing crew, and that's what mattered most.

I remember the threshing season when I was fourteen. I drove our team on a bundle wagon and traveled from farm to farm, following the threshing machine as it made the rounds. I hauled oat bundles from the field to the threshing machine. Once there, I eased the team alongside the giant, dusty machine with pulleys and belts turning this way and that and making a noise so loud I had to yell for someone nearby to hear me.

When the wagon was in place, I motioned to Bill Miller that I was ready, he pulled back the throttle on the Farmall tractor, and the machine came up to full speed. I pitched bundles, one after the other, careful to avoid overlapping them, careful to avoid sending them crosswise into the machine. When a bundle was either crooked or overlapped, the machine growled and shuddered in protest. Bill Miller watched carefully because he knew that too much overlapping of bundles and the machine would stop, its innards plugged.

Bill knew that some bundle pitchers, when they were tired or simply wanted to create a little mischief, plugged the machine. I knew I would catch it from Bill if he thought I was trying to stop the machine on purpose.

After the bundles were unloaded, I looked for a quick drink of water and it was out to the field for another load of bundles. Two other farmers hauled bundles from the field, so the machine never shut down. In addition to the three of us hauling, there were two field pitchers to help load the wagons, one man on the straw stack, another operating the grain sacker, three carrying grain to the granary, and Bill Miller overseeing the tractor and threshing machine. And, of course, a kid shoveling grain in the granary.

Besides swapping stories and pulling tricks on each other (tossing a snake onto a bundle wagon was a common one), the meals were the best of all, especially the noon meals. Farm wives competed to prepare the best spread. Even though there was great rivalry, the women helped each other with preparation and serving. Having an extra dozen or more men for dinner was no small event, especially when they were ravenously hungry.

Threshing day, "Thrashin' day," as many called it, began before dawn for the cook. She had baked several pies, cakes, and a dozen loaves of bread the day before. On threshing day she tried to cook as much as she could on the wood stove before the heat of the day made work in the kitchen near unbearable. She had meat to roast, pork chops to fry, and sauerkraut to bake. She had dill pickles to cut, canned peas and corn to prepare, potatoes to boil, and plates and silverware to lay out on the dinning room table, which was extended to its limit.

Bill Miller would usually give her a little warning. "When this load is off, we'll be in for dinner." She watched out the kitchen window with one eye as the load of oat bundles slowly disappeared into the giant machine that grumbled, shook, and sent chunks of yellow straw onto the stack alongside the barn. When the load was nearly off, she and her helpers carried bowls and platters of steaming food to the table.

Soon we filed into the house after tossing our straw hats in a corner on the porch. It was as if a giant vacuum cleaner had come down on the dining room table. Within minutes, the main course disappeared, and we were eating giant slabs of apple, cherry, and peach pie, huge squares of devil's food cake, all washed down with black coffee from an immense gray pot that sat steaming on a corner of the kitchen stove.

If the threshing took the entire afternoon, and it often did, we filed in for supper, a lesser meal than that served at noon but still of gigantic dimensions.

We moved from farm to farm, from huge meal to huge meal, each cook trying to outdo the previous one—with a few exceptions that we knew about from previous years. We often speeded up operations so that we were required to eat only the minimum number of meals at these places of lesser eating delight.

And then the threshing season was over, the straw piles stood high, and the oat bins ran over—if it had been a good season with ample rains and an absence of storms that felled the crop and made harvesting difficult.

History of Threshing Machines

The first primitive threshing machines were developed in England and Scotland in the mid-1700s. The first American threshing machine was patented in 1791. These early threshing machines were permanently located, water powered, or powered by horses hitched to a special device called a "horse sweep power."

By the early 1820s the fairly reliable Pope Threshing Machine became available. This machine could be moved by wagon and thus hauled from farm to farm rather than having the farmer come to it.

Hiram and John Pitts developed a threshing machine that they patented in 1837. People called the Pope and Pitts machine a "ground hog" thresher. Horses powered it by walking on a treadmill, which was dug into a pit so that the horses walked on an incline. The arrangement gave the appearance of an animal digging into the ground—thus the name ground hog.

Several manufacturers developed threshing machines, but none became as well known as the J. I. Case machine manufactured in Racine, Wisconsin. By the early 1860s, Case's threshing machine was capable of threshing 200 to 300 bushels of grain per day. Early threshing machines were mostly wooden. In 1904 Case introduced the first all-steel thresher, which other manufacturers soon copied.

The grain combine appeared in the 1930s and doomed threshing machines and threshing crews. The combine cut the grain and threshed it too—a combination machine that gave it its name.

Three-Tine Forks

Every farmer remembers a three-tine fork. This simple implement recalls memories of haymows, haystacks, threshing, barn chores, and much more. A farmer used it nearly every day of the year, from forking hay in front of the cattle to helping make a stack during threshing. Most farmers still have at least one.

When I was ten years old, I saw a three-tine fork used for an unusual purpose. I hadn't seen it used that way before, and I haven't seen anyone use it that way since.

Frank Kolka had a Guernsey bull that was mean and hard to handle. I was visiting Frank's sons, Jim and Dave, the day that the bull was out in the barnyard and refused to go back into the barn. Frank had tried everything to persuade the beast to return to his stall, all to no avail. The big brown and white animal pawed the ground, throwing dirt up on his back. He bellowed in that low, menacing way that only a mean bull can. He shook his horns and threatened to hook anyone coming close.

What to do? The bull could not be left in the cow yard, for if he decided to break through the fence, he could do so easily. If he did break out, the problem would be expanded greatly, for a loose bull, particularly a mean one was everyone's nightmare.

George Dietrich, who had recently moved onto the farm across the road from Kolkas, came over to see what all the commotion was about. George had spent all his life in Milwaukee, and Frank was concerned that George might be hurt if the bull crashed through the barnyard fence. But George came over anyway. I figured it was dumb curiosity; being a city fellow, he just didn't know

any better than to tangle with a mad bull.

"See you're having some difficulty with your bull?" George asked. He had a different perspective on farm life than the farmers in our community did. He even talked funny.

"Yeah, we're havin' a terrible time gettin' this damn bull back in the barn," Frank said as he pulled a handkerchief from his pocket and wiped it across his brow. "Better you stay out the way in case he decides to smash through the fence."

"Just might have the solution to your problem," George said.

"You what?" Frank said. I heard it too and couldn't believe that this city guy could possibly know anything about mad bulls.

"I think I know how to return your bull to the barn."

"How?" Frank said rather gruffly.

"You got a three-tine pitchfork?"

"Yeah, I got a three-tine fork."

"Got some old rags?" George asked.

"I think so."

"Little kerosene, too, and a match."

"What in hell you want with all that stuff?" Frank asked.

"You'll see," George said.

Jim and Dave fetched the things Dietrich wanted. George wrapped the rags around the tines of the fork and doused them with kerosene. Then he touched a match to the rags and stepped into the barnyard, keeping his eye on the bull, which was pawing and bellowing on the far side of the yard.

"George, you'll get yourself killed," Frank said. "You sure you know what you're doin?"

"I know perfectly well what I'm doing," George answered.

When he saw George, the bull snorted, bellowed, and pawed a huge clump of dirt over his back. Then he slowly began trotting toward George.

"George, there's still time to climb over the fence!" Frank yelled.

No response from George.

"Boys," Frank motioned to his sons and me, "you'd better stand back in case the bull makes a run at George and smashes through the fence."

We backed up a step or two. None of us wanted to miss what was about to happen in the barnyard.

Black smoke curled up from the kerosene-soaked rag on the end of the three-tine fork. George stood his ground. I couldn't see the expression on his face but wished I could have. I'd never seen a man face a mad bull before.

The bull, now galloping, thundered toward George and his flaming three-tine fork. I could smell the smoke from the burning rags and could see the little cloud of dust kicked up by the bull's hoofs as he ran.

The bull skidded to a stop no more than three feet from the flaming fork that George held motionless in front of him. No one said anything, but Frank Kolka later shared that he was sure that this was the end of his new neighbor. A great hush came over the barnyard. George continued to hold the flaming fork; the bull, his eyes red with meanness, stood staring at George. I wanted to say,

"Do something," but I didn't. I continued watching, waiting, and wondering.

Then the bull took a step forward, stuck his nose on the burning torch, let out a loud snort that could be heard a hundred yards away, turned tail, and trotted into the barn.

"Well I'll be damned," Frank said as he hurried to lock the gate on the bullpen.

We'd all seen a new use for a three-tine fork and gained a powerful measure of respect for our city-bred neighbor, who seemed to know nothing at all about farming, or so we thought.

History of Three-Tine Forks

A three-tine fork is known by various names—pitchfork, hayfork, bundle fork (when it was used during threshing)—but mostly just three-tine fork. It was not a fancy farm implement but consisted of a wooden handle with three slightly curved and sharp tines on the end. Pushed into the ground a few inches, the fork was about as tall as a farm kid old enough to work in the fields.

The three-tine steel fork replaced an earlier wooden model with wooden tines fashioned from a tree limb. In the 1902 *Sears, Roebuck & Company* catalog, you could order a wooden fork that Sears described as, "Unequaled for handling grain of all kinds, straw, flax, clover, etc. Made of hardwood throughout. The widest, lightest and strongest fork made. Forty-five cents."

Wooden forks were used for hundreds of years, before steel forks could be easily manufactured. Steel tines were many times stronger than wooden ones and wore less readily as well. A three-tine fork made of steel lasted for years. The tines shortened with wear; the handle became smooth and worn, but the implement was still serviceable. About all that could happen to a fork was running over it with a wagon and breaking it or trying to lift too much and cracking the handle.

Barbed Wire Fences

Former farm kids remember barbed wire fences, especially Sunday mornings, when the cows got out and the fence had to be fixed before church. They also remember the times they either tried to crawl under one and got caught or stepped over one and snagged their overalls.

Barbed wire fences were once found everywhere, separating farm fields and marking property lines. Fewer barbed wire fences exist today as farming has changed from smaller to larger farms and fewer farmers raise livestock.

Pa and I were putting up a new line fence between our farm and Macijeski's, a modern-day fence with steel fence posts and four strands of barbed wire. The boundary line between our two farms was piled deep with fieldstones that we had each removed from our fields. Work was slow. Stones had to be pushed aside before posts could be placed, and the strands of barbed wire had to be stretched over the rocks from post to post.

Pa insisted the fence be straight—no deviation because a big stone was in the way. We spent more time making things straight than we did pounding posts and stringing wire.

"Don't want the neighbors to talk," Pa said. "Don't want them to think we don't know how to make a straight fence."

All morning we worked through one long, continuous stone pile. It was a hard and tedious job as we shifted stones, pounded posts, strung wire, and made sure everything was absolutely straight. We kept moving, slowly. Until now, when Pa stopped abruptly and jumped back a couple of steps, peering down among the fieldstones.

"Heard something," Pa said. "Strange noise."

"Probably a chipmunk," I said. Lots of chipmunks and other wildlife in these stone piles.

"Wasn't a chipmunk. Different sound than that."

I stopped unwinding barbed wire and listened.

Not a sound along the fence row. It was one of those warm, windless days in spring when sound traveled great distances.

"Where'd the noise come from?" I asked.

"Right here. Right in front of me, from that pile of rocks."

"Could have come from across the road," I said. "Sound travels on a day like this."

"Didn't come from across the road. Sound came from right there." Pa pointed with the handle of the sledgehammer.

Then we both heard it. A dry, rattling sound. A hollow, frightful noise.

"Rattlesnake," Pa yelled as he bounded off the stone pile, leaving behind the sledgehammer.

"Climb up on a tractor tire," he yelled. "Snake can't crawl up a rubber tire."

Our Farmall H tractor had tall tires in the back, the kind with deep lugs. Pa stood on one, and I stood on the other, both of us peering into the stone pile for a glimpse of the rattler that we knew was there.

Pa was sure he had spotted it and that the snake was chasing him. I told him I hadn't seen a snake come out of the stone pile. But the look on Pa's face suggested he wasn't too sure about that. After all, I hadn't even heard the snake rattle the first time.

It seemed like an hour that we stood on the tractor tires—I'm sure it wasn't nearly that long, listening for more rattles and a glimpse of a rattler that must have lived in the stones and was waking up from a long winter's rest. Finally, Pa stepped down from the tire, grabbed up a steel fence post, and slowly advanced on the stone pile.

"I wanna get the sledgehammer," he whispered. "Then we'll get out of here."

He slowly and carefully reached for the sledgehammer handle, moving in slow motion, deliberate with each step. Then he grabbed the sledge and ran back to the trailer, tossing the hammer in among the wire and posts. He climbed on the tractor seat, and we roared off across the field. I was certain he thought the rattlesnake was right behind us and probably gaining.

Two weeks later we returned to making fence in the stone pile next to Macijeski's. We worked gingerly, alert to any sound or movement. We finished putting up the fence without incident.

History of Barbed Wire Fences

The story of barbed wire begins at an 1873 county fair in DeKalb, Illinois. Henry Rose, a local farmer, was showing off his recent invention, a wooden strip to which he had fastened metal points. The strip was fastened to a wooden fence, and because of the sharp points, livestock didn't rub on the fence boards and break them.

Joseph Glidden, another area farmer, examined this new invention and thought he could apply the same concept to wire, which was less expensive to buy and transport and easier to install than wood.

Glidden returned to his farm and spent several days figuring out how to twist wire strands to which he tied barbs. Glidden strung this new "barbed wire" around his farm and soon drew the attention of his neighbors. They asked him to make barbed wire for them, which he did during the winter months.

Meanwhile, Isaac Ellwood, a DeKalb hardware store owner, had seen the display at the county fair and had learned about Glidden's invention. Another DeKalb merchant, Jacob Haish, a lumber dealer, also became interested, and he as well as Glidden submitted applications to the U.S. Patent

Office. A debate developed over which man should be credited with inventing barbed wire as each developed a slightly different design. Officially, Glidden was given the nod. The Patent Office granted him a patent on November 24, 1874.

After he received his patent, Glidden offered hardware store owner Elwood half-interest in his invention and production rights for $265. They named the partnership the Barb Wire Fence Company and sold the wire through Elwood's DeKalb hardware store. They sold five tons of fencing in 1874 and by 1880 were selling more than 40 tons yearly. In 1876 Glidden sold his half-interest to a Massachusetts-based wire company for $60,000, plus 25 cents for every 100 pounds of wire manufactured.

Dr. Daryl Watson, Director of the Jo-Daviess County Museum and Historical Society in Galena, Illinois, said barbed wire symbolizes the changes occurring in agriculture. Before barbed wire, from settlement days to the 1870s, much of the Midwest was a wheat-growing region. Beginning in the 1870s, wheat gave way to dairy and beef farming, corn and oats, and often chickens and hogs—diversified farming, it was called. Barbed wire fences appeared, and farms were divided into fields where cattle grazed and where corn, hay, and other crops were grown.

In some parts of the Midwest, by the 1970s, crop farming replaced dairy and livestock. The barbed wire fences came down so that farmers with big tractors could more easily work. By noting present and former wire fence lines, one can identify regional farming trends, according to Dr. Watson.

Dairy Cows

The humble dairy cow, quietly chewing her cud while standing in a green hillside pasture, is a reminder of what farming was once like in many parts of the country, when almost every farmer owned a few cows. Today fewer farms have dairy cows, and they are seldom seen grazing in green pastures. Yet dairy cows remain a symbol of rural life, of a more peaceful time, of quiet and contentment.

Josephine was a good-looking Holstein cow, more black than white, alert ears, strong legs. She was obedient, too. Took her stall in the barn without encouragement, always ate her hay and silage, never knew a sick day as far as I knew. She was four or five years old, in her prime, and she gave lots of milk. Filled a sixteen-quart pail every milking. You'd think Josephine was the kind of cow any farmer would love to have in his barn. Except Josephine had a quirk. It didn't much bother Josephine, but it was surely a problem for the person milking, who was always Pa.

When asked about Josephine, Pa would mumble something about her being ticklish or maybe simply ornery—it depended on the day you asked.

Here is what would happen about every week or so. There was no predicting the event—sometimes an entire week would go by and all was well. I would milk my cows and Pa would milk his and all was calm and content.

Then I would hear this "Ka-bang!" and see Pa's milk pail sail out into the alley behind the cows, splashing milk all over the concrete floor. Pa's reaction was always the same after he picked himself up from the straw.

"I'm gonna sell that damn cow the first chance I get!"

He spoke in a voice loud enough to startle the rest of the cows in the lineup.

This went on for awhile, to my amusement, but it wasn't funny for Pa and became less so as the weeks passed. He always thought she'd get over her problem. Maybe she was a little ticklish, and maybe she had a streak of orneriness. Most cows get over these characteristics with time. Pa was patient, to a point.

One day a cattle dealer came by, as happened from time to time.

"Got any good cows for sale, Herman?" he asked.

"I do," Pa said. They were both leaning on the barnyard fence, looking at the cows. My twin brothers and I stood nearby.

"That big Holstein over there gives a lot of milk, eats well, but I'm running out of room in the barn and I'm gonna have to let her go," Pa said with nary a smile on his face.

"Good lookin' cow," the dealer said.

"She is that," Pa answered.

"You say she gives a lot of milk?"

"She does, right now about sixteen quarts a milking."

"That much?"

"Yup."

"What"ll you take for her?" the dealer asked.

"Should be worth three hundred dollars."

"Give you two and a half."

"She's yours," Pa said. Pa and the dealer went in the house to settle up; my brothers and I stayed outside. Soon my twin brothers began to sing, "Pa sold the kicker cow, Pa sold the kicker cow."

The dealer on his way to the car heard the little ditty.

"What are those kids singing?" he asked

"Oh, it's some little song. Those kids are always making up songs. You know how kids are."

The dealer drove away, and long after the dust on the road past the farm settled, Pa had not yet finished pointing out to my brothers how they had almost lost a sale for him. No one was sorry to see Josephine leave the farm when a cattle truck came for her the next day.

History of Dairy Cows

Dairy cows have been in the United States since Colonial days. The black and white Holstein cow, so popular in the major dairy states of Wisconsin, California, and New York, came with the Dutch when they settled New Amsterdam (now New York) in 1630. Jerseys, smaller and fawn-colored, are the second most popular breed but are far outnumbered by Holsteins. Jerseys arrived from the Jersey Isles in 1850.

Milking Shorthorns, earlier called Durhams because they originated in County Durham, England, were brought to this country in 1783. Durham cows were often the ones seen following the pioneer wagons as they moved West. They were multipurpose animals: settlers milked them, butchered them for meat, and hitched them to their farm implements.

Other dairy breeds include the Brown Swiss from Switzerland, Guernsey from the Isle of Guernsey, and Ayrshire from Scotland.

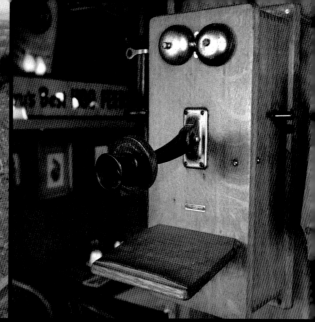

Depots and Trains

Depots stand as reminders of the golden years of the railroad that brought immigrants to the Midwest, hauled wheat, carried lumber, and above all, made communities more accessible to the outside world. Physical isolation had long been a characteristic of many rural communities. The railroad with its depots changed all that.

It is not difficult to locate former depots. Today they are historical museums, restaurants, chamber of commerce offices, resting places for bicyclists (some former rail lines are bike trails), and business establishments. A few of these interesting buildings still serve the trains that pass through rural communities.

I remember the steam locomotive whistle as the engine lumbered along the tracks from the West, from Marshfield on its way to Fond du Lac with many stops along the way, whistling at every road crossing, long and short blasts. It was an exciting sound, especially for a farm boy who had never ridden on a train but who had watched locomotives with their long ribbons of cars pulling into the depot in town.

Two passenger trains came each day, one traveling east, one traveling west, plus several freight trains. The three-room depot was a busy place. One room was the depot agent's office, where the telegraph equipment was located along with a huge wooden desk and a small black stove. Next to it was a larger room, the passenger waiting area with wooden benches and railroad schedules nailed to otherwise bare walls. Another, larger coal stove stood in the middle of this room, with a shuttle of black coal next to it. The freight room, the third room in the depot, faced south. Everything that came to the village—groceries, dry goods, bananas, furniture and coffins for Jones' furniture store, stoves for Hotz Hardware, and horseshoes for Christenson's blacksmith shop—came to the depot. Everything necessary for the operation of a village and the farms surrounding it came on the train, for there were no trucks to haul supplies, and horses and wagons were too slow.

The whistle sounded again, much louder now. I clutched my mother's hand and continued to look down the tracks where they veered west and followed the Pine River Valley out of town. I could see the smoke before I saw the engine, black smoke that lifted above the treetops and trailed off with the wind. Then the locomotive burst into view, clearly the largest, most frightening, most exciting machine a small boy ever saw. The locomotive whistle sounded again in a cloud of steam and smoke, and I jumped, for the sound was so much louder than I imagined. I hadn't been this close to a train before, and now I was standing on the passenger platform at the depot, along with several other people. We all were taking the Chicago Northwestern train to Fond du Lac, where we could change trains and go anywhere, nearly anywhere in the country.

History of Depots and Trains

From Civil War days until the 1950s, railroad depots were the center of activity in most villages and cities. For towns not on a river or large body of water, the depot and the train tied them to the outside world. At the depot one could see travelers, people who had come from far distant places like Chicago or St. Louis or Minneapolis. Traveling salesmen, selling everything from pianos to anvils, from coffins to cash registers, rode the rails. Families off to visit relatives, young men and women looking for work in a new place or merely looking for a new place, traveled the trains. Crooks, thieves, con artists, and gamblers sometimes rode from town to town, looking for a "soft touch."

Most village depots included only the necessities. They had no indoor plumbing—men's and women's outhouses were located in the back. The depot provided a place to wait and keep warm.

The first railroads and depots came to the Midwest after the 1850s, and by the 1960s, many trains, tracks, and depots had disappeared. Depots and trains were magical for farm boys and girls who seldom saw people from the outside world, who wondered what it was like in the city, who wondered how the people looked and how they talked, what kind of shoes they wore, and how many wore bib overalls.

Rural Mail Carriers

Rural mail carriers continue to make their rounds, every day, all seasons. Country people look forward to their pulling up to the mailboxes as much today as they did when the first mail carrier came by, driving a team of horses. Some people claim that Rural Free Delivery (RFD) was the second most important innovation (after the railroad), linking farmers with the outside world. With RFD, a farmer could receive mail every day, delivered to a mailbox at the end of his driveway. Previously he received mail only when he picked it up at a nearby village post office, often located in a country store.

I'd found the tent in the Sears catalog and convinced my mother that I should order it, that it was something I desperately needed. I had saved the $9.89, which the tent cost, from my potato-picking money and bought a money order at the post office. I filled out the order form, put the envelope in the mailbox, and slid up the red flag telling the mail carrier that there was mail to pick up.

It was summer and school vacation, so I arranged my work so that I could watch for the mailman. Promptly at eleven o' clock, I spotted the cloud of dust telling me that

Clarence Corning and his blue Dodge were coming down the road, making the stops along Rural Route 1. He would soon arrive at our shiny white mailbox, R.R. 65.

I figured it would take a couple of days for my order to arrive in Chicago, a day for them to fill the order, and a couple days for the return trip. Five days later I watched earnestly for the dust and the blue Dodge. I did this for three days, and nothing, no package from Sears, no new tent.

Each day I thought about this wonderful tent: big

enough so that my brothers and I could sleep in it in the woods under some oak trees. I would build a campfire in front of the tent, and we would watch the flames and I'd repeat the stories I had read in *Outdoor Life* magazine about frontiersmen and the tents they had, and when necessary, I'd add to the stories to make them scarier.

Two days later Mr. Corning stopped at our mailbox, and when I raced down to pick up the mail, I found a letter from Sears. No package, just a thin letter.

I ripped it open. "We are sorry to inform you that your tent is not available at this time. We should have a new supply and will mail one to you as soon as possible."

Everyday, I watched for the blue Dodge. Some days Mr. Corning waved at me as he drove by. No mail for us. Other days he left a magazine or the weekly newspaper, but no word from Sears. No package containing a wonderful tent designed for someone who loved the outdoors and wanted to sleep in the woods.

Finally, after three weeks of watching and waiting, another thin letter from Sears arrived. "We regret to inform you that the tent you ordered, Number A365, is no longer available. We are returning your money order."

Our mailman was well known as a carrier of news good and bad. No matter which it was, we still looked for his coming every day.

History of Rural Mail Carriers

Farmers, especially those who were active members of the Grange (a national farm organization), lobbied for free mail delivery starting in the late 1800s. A Georgia congressman, Tom Watson, drafted legislation for a permanent rural free delivery in 1893. Congress approved the proposal, but the then-postmaster general rejected it. Reintroduced, RFD became law in 1896. In that year the first five official rural delivery routes began operating in Jefferson County, West Virginia. By 1899 forty states had rural delivery routes.

Once the rural mail carrier started making rounds, farmers began subscribing to magazines and to daily and weekly newspapers. No longer was news from the outside world a week or more late. They also began receiving mail-order catalogs such as Sears, Roebuck and Montgomery Ward; they could order goods from the catalog and have them delivered to their door. Before RFD, catalog orders were delivered to the local railroad depot.

Dick Paisley was an Iowa rural mail carrier for 27½ years. He started a mail route in 1952 and retired in 1979. In his eighties, slim and wiry and not beyond slipping in an occasional cuss word, Paisley recalled the days spent on his mail route. He drove the only rural route out of Holy Cross, Iowa, where he had 432 customers.

He arrived at the post office every morning at 7 a.m., Monday through Saturday, sorted the mail, and left the post office about 9:30 to deliver mail. He completed his route and was back in the post office between 2:30 and 3:00 each afternoon.

Rural mail carriers depended on their cars. Paisley said, "I'd trade cars twice a year. I'd have around 20,000 miles when I'd trade. Half of my route was dirt road. The car was pretty shot when I traded it. I had a 100-mile mail route. When I first started, it was 45 miles. I carried two spares; you always got nails on the roads around here. Sometimes, when changing a tire, the brakes would be so hot you couldn't take the lug nuts off."

Winter and spring were the worst times on the mail route, winter because of the snowdrifts and spring because of the mud. Paisley developed some unique approaches for dealing with these challenges.

He explained how to drive through a snowdrift. "You drive up to it, check it out, back up, and figure out how fast you should hit it." He said his system usually worked; the trick was hitting the snowdrift at the right speed.

Paisley also had a system for handling muddy roads.

He explained, "One spring it was especially muddy. I was driving a 1963 Chevrolet. I took it over to Danny Ball's repair shop, and I said, "You weld me a steel plate from the front bumper to back behind the transmission." He said, "You won't be able to change your oil or grease it." I said, "That's all right I don't plan to do that before I trade it off anyway." So he did; he welded this sheet of steel under the car. It was like a flat-bottomed boat, that's what it was like. I'd drive up to a mud hole, look at it, and figure out how much speed I'd need. It didn't take me long to learn to slide her across.

"One day I'm on this back road and Sly Hess has an M tractor hitched to a manure spreader and he's stuck in the middle of the road. He's got a Ford tractor in front of the M—trying to pull him out. I come along and there's fifteen farmers standing there.

"Can't get through, Dick," they say.

"Yeah, I can get through." I put the mail in the box and I say, "Just get out the way, cause you're gonna get wet."

"Gonna get wet?"

"Yeah, all that water's comin' out of that hole. So I set the windshield wipers, backed down the road, and I hit the gas. I hung on to the steering wheel real good cause I couldn't see a damn thing. I slid the car right across the hole and drove on down the road. People couldn't figure out how I did it."

Telephones

Today, telephones are taken for granted, but the memories of the early ones before push-button and cordless models remain. These early telephones were primitive by today's standards, but they were clearly wonderful devices for rural people, who were often isolated from their neighbors.

It was only a single ring, which meant somebody on our line was trying to reach Central.

My brothers and I were home alone on a Saturday afternoon, and my brother Don picked up the phone to listen. We were admonished never to listen in on other people's calls, and we never did when Ma and Pa were around. But we always picked up the phone when they were gone. Among the three of us, we pledged never to tattle that we were doing this—as long as the kid who was listening would share every word. It was Don's turn to listen in. Darrel and I gathered nearby.

"Who is it?" I whispered.

Don pushed me away, signaling that I should remain quiet.

"Who is it?" I whispered again.

Don covered up the mouthpiece on the phone and turned to face Darrel and me.

"It's Jim Kolka," Don said.

"Who's he talking to?" Darrel asked.

"Some girl."

"A girl?" I asked.

"Yes, a girl. Now keep quiet so I can hear."

Kolkas had just had a phone put in and I wondered if Jim knew that others on the party line could listen in on conversations.

"What's he saying?" Darrel asked.

Don covered the mouthpiece again and began chuckling.

"Well, what's he saying?" I asked.

"He's asking this girl for a date," Don said. He couldn't control his laughter.

"A date?" I said.

"Yeah, and he's stumbling and mumbling and having a heck of a time spitting out the words," Don said.

"Bet he doesn't think anyone is listening in," Darrel added. We were all three laughing, now.

Don continued listening, and then he said into the mouthpiece, "Jim, you're gonna have to do better than that or you'll never get a date." Then he hung up quickly.

The three of us bent over with laughter. We knew what we had done was a dirty trick, but what a wonderful one it was. Not long after that we saw Jim in school. "Say, was one of you guys listening in on the phone the other day?"

"One of us? Nah, our Ma doesn't let us do that."

History of Telephones

Alexander Graham Bell invented the telephone in 1876, calling it an "electrical speech machine." Bell, who was born in Edinburgh, Scotland, in 1847, came to this country and settled in Boston. One of his interests was the education of the hearing impaired. He had been experimenting with sound amplification when he stumbled onto the idea of the telephone. Like so many new inventions, Bell's telephone was viewed as a "passing fancy," especially by the telegraph people, who, by the late 1800s, had a monopoly on town-to-town communication.

With a telephone, farmers didn't have to drive to a train depot to send a message; the telephone came to their farm, and the instrument hung on the wall in the kitchen or the dining room. The telephone soon was widely accepted by nearly everyone. Telephone companies began springing up throughout the country; the first one started in Noblesville, Indiana, in 1894.

Some farmers complained about the costs for telephones, but almost none had them removed. They had become essential parts of life.

Mail-Order Catalogs

Many farm homes had only two books: the Holy Bible and the Sears catalog. One ministered to the soul; the other satisfied nearly every other human need. Even in homes with other books, the mail-order catalog was the only one with pictures. Today the Sears, Roebuck and Montgomery Ward catalogs are gone, but what wonderful memories they provide.

My brothers and I started looking for it in early November. Each afternoon when we got home from school, we asked, "Did it come today?"

"No, not today," Ma said with a little smile. She knew what we were waiting for. We were waiting for the Sears, Roebuck Christmas catalog, that wonderful display of everything we could ever want. On the colorful pages of this book, we found board games, toy guns, books, farm sets, toy cars (some so big that you could sit inside and pedal), card games like Flinch and Old Maid, Lincoln Logs, and Tinker Toys.

We thumbed the pages of the catalog (Sears called it a Wish Book) by the wood stove in the dining room, with the light of a kerosene lamp flickering on the pages.

Ma said we could pick out one toy and one practical thing like a sweater or a winter cap. The Sears Christmas catalog had pages of clothing: heavy wool plaid coats (Mackinaws, Pa called them), leather mittens with wool liners, wool pants so heavy that the wind couldn't penetrate them, winter caps, and sweaters. There was long underwear of various designs: one-piece and two-piece, all wool, and those with wool and cotton blends. I never

requested wool underwear because it itched and crawled. Let the temperature in a room rise beyond seventy degrees, and the underwear felt like the beginning of a poison ivy attack. The more I moved, the more the wool underwear crept up my ankles as though it had come alive. I knew it was happening when I felt a cold draft blowing up my leg.

My brothers and I spent days deciding what we wanted and then changing our minds for something different. For my toy, I usually selected a book, but the problem was deciding which one. The catalog had many from which to choose. Finally, the day came when we had to decide, and Ma would fill out the order form. Then came the long wait till Christmas morning.

History of Mail-Order Catalogs

The mail-order catalog business dates back to the 1860s and 1870s, but these were often specialty catalogs, usually manufacturers selling their own products. The first general-merchandise, mail-order catalog is credited to Aaron Montgomery Ward, who began Montgomery Ward & Co. in Chicago in 1872.

Ward's first catalog, printed in 1871, was a single-page price list that he planned to send farmer members of the National Grange of the Patrons of Husbandry. But the horrendous Chicago fire that burned much of the downtown in the fall of 1871 destroyed his business before it got started. Ward endured and in 1872 began distributing his catalog listing 163 items.

Richard Warren Sears, who was born in Stewartville, Minnesota, learned telegraphy while he was still in his teens and became a station agent at North Redwood, Minnesota. In 1886 a local jeweler refused a shipment of watches. The shipper offered them on consignment to Sears, and soon he was ordering more watches for resale by other railroad station agents. In a few months Sears quit the railroad and established a full-time mail-order business in Minneapolis called the R.W. Sears Watch Company. In 1887 he moved the business to Chicago to take advantage of its more central location and better transportation facilities. The first Sears catalog appeared in 1891 and included 32 pages of watches and an 8-page insert displaying jewelry and sewing machines.

Soon after Sears arrived in Chicago, Alvah Curtis Roebuck answered Sears' ad for a watchmaker. Thus began the connection of Sears and Roebuck. In 1893 the name Sears, Roebuck & Company was established. In that year their catalog had 200 pages and included a broad line of merchandise. By 1908 the catalog contained 1,184 pages.

Many families received both Wards and Sears catalogs in their rural mail boxes. At the turn of the century, a farmer or his wife could order water pumps, guitars and accordions, corsets, fruit trees, shotguns, women's unmentionables, dresses, men's suits, books, toys, and much more.

In 1909 Sears began selling houses through their catalog, including building plans, lumber, nails, and paint—everything that was needed for building a home. By the 1920s Sears offered 80 different home models, costing from less than $1,000 to one selling for about $5,000. In 1934 the Depression forced Sears to stop selling houses; but thousands were sold during the 25 years they were available, and many remain standing today.

Some readers looked to their catalogs for even more than the merchandise offered. Sears once received the following letter from a Tennessee farmer:

"Dear Sir: I thought I would write you a line as I am looking for a wife. I want a good cook and a clean woman. I am 24 years old and I want a girl my age. If you can look for me a wife I will pay you for your trouble as I am lonely and would like to be married."

It wasn't only farm men who were looking for spouses. An Idaho woman sent a letter to Sears along with a catalog illustration of a handsome man. She wrote: "I am a lonely school teacher in the dismal hills of Idaho. Would you be kind enough to do your share in assisting a poor forlorn teacher in her future happiness by sending this man which you advertised in your latest edition?"

Most catalogs were recycled. Once a new catalog arrived, the outdated one found its way to the outhouse and was used as a ready source of toilet paper.

Montgomery Ward closed its mail-order catalog operations in 1985; Sears, Roebuck and Company published its last catalog in 1993.

Box Cameras

Almost everyone has a photo album filled with photographs taken at family reunions, Thanksgiving and Christmas gatherings, at summer picnics, and during visits of city relatives. These are memories of an earlier day, many of them captured with a Kodak box camera. The box camera made everyone a photographer; taking pictures had been only for professionals before its invention.

On my third birthday, Ma dressed me in my best bib overalls and a freshly washed shirt. She said I should wear my straw hat and come outside the house.

"I want to take your picture," she said. She had her box camera and was moving me around so that I was standing with the sun shining square in my face.

"Don't squint," she said. I couldn't avoid it. I tried to keep my eyes open while she stared down into the black box.

"Ready?"

I said that I was.

"Smile." I screwed up a little smirk.

She pushed the shutter and that was that. A couple weeks later, she showed me the photo she'd taken. It had come out just fine, even though I had squinted.

Ma's photo album was full of my pictures, starting when I was a baby. There were pictures of me with my teddy bear, with my wagon, with my wheelbarrow, dressed up for church, by the Christmas tree, and next to one of Pa's best cows.

Then everything changed. My twin brothers were born. Now the box camera came out to take a picture of those "cute twins." If I was asked to be in a picture, they were always in it, too.

"Don't stand in front of the twins," Ma said. "Got to see those cute twins." I cowered in the background, behind the buggy, or off to the side someplace. I was in the picture, but I wasn't. Relatives began asking, "Who is that kid with those cute twins?" I didn't know whether they were kidding or serious.

I began wishing Ma didn't have her old box camera. It was becoming embarrassing. Once I was the star of all the photos; now I was scarcely a bit player. Life could be cruel, and a box camera contributed to the cruelty.

History of Box Cameras

Photo images have been known since the late 18th century, when Britain's Sir Humphrey Davey experimented with them. These early images were not permanent, and the photo turned black when exposed to light.

By the1860s, professional photographers with their huge plate film cameras and darkrooms traveled the country making photographs. At that time photography was sufficiently complex that only professionals could do it.

A dramatic breakthrough occurred in the early 1880s, when George Eastman invented a film consisting of a long strip of paper coated with light-sensitive emulsion. By 1888, Eastman was rolling the paper onto a spool and the highly portable box camera with the ability to take several photos became possible. Eastman, who started the Eastman Kodak Company, invented a film roll holder adaptable to nearly every plate camera on the market. Eastman continued working toward simplifying photography so that everyone could do it.

The first Kodak camera came on the market in 1888, and soon thousands of them were sold. This early camera came preloaded with enough film for 100 exposures. It was priced at $25. After use, the camera was mailed back to Rochester, New York, where the company developed the film, made prints, and inserted new film.

By 1896 Eastman had sold 100,000 Kodak cameras. The company was making roll film at the rate of 400 miles a month. Kodak's motto in those days was, "You push the button—we do the rest."

A pocket model Kodak sold for $5.00 in the late 1800s, but Kodak was working toward producing an even less expensive model. In 1900 Kodak introduced the first Brownie camera, which sold for $1 and was guaranteed to operate simply and efficiently. A long line of highly successful Brownie cameras followed this early one. A popular Brownie box camera was Model 2A, which sold for $4.58 in 1920. It used number 116 film, with 12 exposures and sold for 60 cents per roll. The photos were 2 1/4 by 1 1/4 inches, vertical or horizontal format. The camera was black, 6 inches deep, 7 inches high, and 3 1/2 inches wide, with a retractable carrying handle. It was small enough to carry nearly everywhere.

George Eastman created the amateur photographer. No longer did people travel to photo studios to have their pictures taken or arrange for a traveling photographer to visit their farm, as some rural people did. The Kodak box camera stood on the shelf, waiting for a moment when someone grabbed it and snapped a photo—at a birthday, during threshing, of the first tractor, of a favorite cow, of a hundred happenings. Everyone was a photographer, and the professionals were relegated to studios, newspapers, and magazines.

Radios

Radios helped bring rural and urban people together. Farmers heard the same national news, the same music, and the same comedy programs that their city cousins heard. The radio also helped farmers keep up-to-date on market happenings and university agriculture research. All of this was free, except for the cost of the radio and batteries—and the patience to listen to commercials selling everything from Red Brand fencing (Keystone Steel and Wire company) to Wheaties, Lux Soap, Crisco, Lava Soap, Pepsi-Cola, and Ovaltine.

At first all I heard was a little static when I snapped on our Philco battery-operated radio. Every afternoon, after my chores were done—the wood boxes filled, the chickens fed, and the eggs picked—I could listen to "my stories." I was there, with my heroes, living high adventure through the radio.

I heard the announcer's voice and pulled my chair a little closer. I was listening to *Captain Midnight*, one of my favorite programs where the bad guys were captured, the good guys were saved, and everything came out all right by the end of each segment. The program was sponsored by Ovaltine, a powdered chocolate-like flavoring to mix with milk. I convinced Ma that I absolutely needed to drink Ovaltine, at least three jars of it. If I sent in three jar labels, I would receive a genuine decoder ring. I never told Ma that I didn't like Ovaltine-flavored milk. I drank a glassful every meal, trying to smile as I did. I had to have the decoder ring. It was impossible to grasp the entire meaning of each Captain Midnight show without decoding the message at the end.

Finally, the second jar of Ovaltine was empty, and I urged Ma to buy the third and last one so that I could send in the labels. I filled out the little form and mailed it all in. And I waited. Program after program went by, and I missed the important message at the end because I didn't have a decoder ring.

After a month, a little box arrived in the mail. I tore the box open and it was my ring. A shiny gold and blue ring that could be adjusted to fit my finger. I slipped it on, hardly able to wait until evening and the *Captain Midnight* show.

When the show was over, the announcer read the secret numbers and I copied them on a sheet of paper. After some struggle and adjustment of my special decoder ring, I figured out the message and wrote it down: "Drink more Ovaltine." Some message. I didn't even like the stuff. I continued listening to *Captain Midnight* but with far less enthusiasm. I wore my decoder ring until it turned my finger green; then I put it away with my other important things.

History of Radios

Radio history began in 1895, when Guglielmo Marconi, a self-taught Italian inventor, experimented with sending radio signals. Radio experiments took place in the United States as well, building on Marconi's pioneering efforts.

In 1920 Westinghouse built a 100-watt commercial radio station on top of a factory in Pittsburgh, and KDKA came on the air. Other radio stations soon followed. By 1922, 537 radio stations were broadcasting in the United States. About 100,000 radio sets were manufactured in 1922, 500,000 in 1923. Prices soon began dropping; therefore, average people could afford a set.

Several kinds of radio programs emerged. News programs immediately became popular. Many people remember President Franklin Delano Roosevelt's speech to Congress on December 8, 1941: "Yesterday, December 7, 1941, a date that will live in infamy, the United States of America was suddenly and deliberately attacked by naval and air forces of the Empire of Japan."

Many radio broadcasts were designed for farmers: early morning and noon market news, information from university researchers, and weather information. Radio stations such as WHA at the University of Wisconsin broadcast agricultural information. WHA also broadcast special programs on music, art, and nature appreciation to the one-room country schools scattered throughout the region.

Everyone enjoyed radio comedy shows: *Amos and Andy, Fred Allen, Burns and Allen, Bob Hope, Lum n' Abner, Jack Benny and Mary Livingston, Red Skelton, Milton Berle, Edgar Bergen and Charlie McCarthy, The Great Gildersleeve, The Life of Riley, The Aldrich Family, and of course Fibber McGee and Molly.* No one wanted to miss Fibber McGee opening his overcrowded closet and having everything tumble out on the floor (the wonders of sound effects) on nearly every show.

For the children, adventure shows were broadcast every afternoon with heroes like *Jack Armstrong, The Lone Ranger, Tom Mix, Terry and the Pirates, The Green Hornet, Sky King, Hopalong Cassidy, Tarzan, and Sergeant Preston* (with his lead dog King), and *Captain Midnight.*

Radio broadcast Friday night fights—Jack Dempsey and Gene Tunney, Joe Louis and Max Schmeling. There were music programs, such as *The Guy Lombardo Show, Kraft Music Hall,* and *Your Hit Parade.* And variety shows, *Arthur Godfrey's Talent Scouts, The Ed Sullivan Show,* and *Major Bowes' Original Amateur Hour. The National Barn Dance* began broadcasting on WLS (Chicago) in 1924 and continued until 1960. *The Grand Ole' Opry* came on the air in 1925 from Nashville, Tennessee, and continues on television.

During daytime hours, radio broadcast soap operas—*The Romance of Helen Trent, Ma Perkins, Backstage Wife,* and *Our Gal Sunday.*

Evening drama programs drew thousands of listeners to their radios: *Gangbusters, The FBI in Peace and War, Death Valley Days,* and *The Shadow,* with Orson Wells playing the lead part.

Farmers had radios long before electricity came to their farms. With battery power and an antenna stretched from the radio set to the windmill, farmers could pick up a few stations.

Early radio had something for everyone—drama, music, comedy, children's programs, news, weather, farm market reports. It was a welcome addition to rural communities.

PART IV: COMMUNITY

Country Taverns

Cussed and discussed, country taverns have been a part of many rural communities since settlement days They served as gathering places and community centers, and they were a rich source of stories. Like many ma-and-pa businesses, they are disappearing, but memories of them remain.

Pa didn't like taverns. He made it clear to my brothers and me that we should never set foot in one, ever. For any reason. We had several taverns in our town, interesting places, I thought. Loud sounds came from them when I walked by on a Saturday night—laughter, men's voices, sometimes music. And exotic smells sifted out onto the sidewalk—smells unknown to a country boy accustomed to rich and earthy aromas.

One time I got enough nerve to ask Pa why he was so down on taverns. They were surely popular places in my hometown. I knew he wasn't against drinking—we usual-ly had a few bottles of beer in the icebox and a spare case in the cellar.

"You'll end up like Clem Woodward."

Everybody knew Clem. He drove a Model-A Ford and spent every Saturday night in the tavern. I didn't see much wrong with that, especially since his wife had died and his kids had long ago left the farm. Saturday night was a chance for him to chat with other farmers, find out what was going on, and swap a few stories. He drove home every Saturday night in a rather unusual way. His top speed was never more than twenty-five miles an hour, and he steered from one side of the dirt road to the other all the way home. When he sensed he was headed for the ditch, he cranked the steering wheel over and then, of course, was headed for the opposite ditch. People here knew that Clem left for home shortly after midnight, and they stayed off the road that he took. No one wanted to meet Clem Woodward driving home from the tavern. The rest of the week Clem was sober and tended to his farming.

On Sunday mornings, Pa never failed to point out to my brothers and me Clem's Model-A tracks along the road. They were interesting tracks to be sure, had sort of an artistic pattern to them, I thought. I never mentioned this to Pa, though. He wanted me to see this "trail of drunkenness," as he called it, and I did many times. He thought the tracks were sufficient evidence for never entering a tavern. I was not convinced.

History of Country Taverns

James Leary, folklorist at the University of Wisconsin-Madison, wrote, "Throughout the state's history, Wisconsin taverns have sustained the legacy of old world inns, of cultural institutions sharing status with, and often numerically exceeding, churches." The same could be said about taverns in many other states.

Country taverns were and are family gathering places. An example is Breitbach's, which claims to be the oldest tavern In Iowa. It's found in Balltown, population 39. Breitbach's opened in 1852, by a federal permit issued from President Millard Fillmore. Jacob Breitbach came from Germany in 1826 and purchased the tavern on July 17, 1863, for $145 at a sheriff's sale. Jacob was the great-great-grandfather of the present owner, Mike Breitbach.

In the early days the place was a roadhouse and stagecoach stop on the trail from Dubuque to Guttenberg, going north along the Mississippi. Today it's a tavern and popular restaurant.

Farmers and everyone else in the community came together at this tavern. "In the early days, women were not allowed in bars. There were backrooms for the women and children," Breitbach said. "We once had a grocery store as part of the building, and that's where the women and children would go."

German Catholics were the predominant ethnic group in this southeastern Iowa community. On Sundays they went to church and afterward stopped at the tavern, a common event in many German communities. They came to drink, to discuss community and national events, and to share information with each other—who needed a hired hand, who was sick, who had a horse for sale.

The tavern faced closing in 1933, when Prohibition ended (It had stayed open during Prohibition years). The state of Iowa passed a law that for a beer license to be granted, the tavern must be in an incorporated village or city. Balltown, then with a population of 22, never was considered large enough to incorporate. But incorporate it did, at a meeting in the tavern. Breitbach said, "They got themselves a mayor and five councilmen; the meetings were here, and they met once a year." Over the years, residents of Balltown have taken turns serving as mayor and councilmen.

Breitbach's grandfather was a conservative German who wouldn't spend money unless absolutely necessary. "We didn't get indoor plumbing until 1970; he would never spend the money. We had outside toilets. Dad was on him all the time to put in plumbing," Breitbach said. His answer, 'Why should we change now?' We did have electricity for refrigeration (coming in 1940 or 1941) with a minimum bill of $4.50 a month. You had to pay that amount even if you didn't use it. Many months, he'd use only $2 worth, and it would make him so mad; but that's the way it was."

The country tavern played an important role in rural America and in many communities continues to do so.

Gristmills

To find an old gristmill, look for a millpond. Thousands of these old mills are sprinkled across the Midwest. Standing near one, you can almost hear the banter of farmers unloading their grain and sharing stories. You can picture the miller, his clothes covered with white dust, pushing a lever here and pulling a handle there, all the while talking with his farmer customers. And you can feel the building shudder as the turbine turns and the mill grinds.

Every couple weeks Pa took the back seat out of our 1936 Plymouth and loaded the space with gunny bags filled with cob corn and oats. And we were on our way to the mill to have the grain ground into cow feed, or grist, as it was called.

When we arrived, Pa backed the Plymouth to the unloading platform, where we lifted the sacks of corn and oats up to the miller, who hoisted them the rest of the way. The mill was a busy place where farmers from throughout the area brought their grain for grinding. As they waited, they talked about their cows, the weather, crops, fishing, and politics. They told stories. They laughed and kidded each other.

If it was winter and bitterly cold, we all crowded into the miller's tiny office, where he kept a little wood stove going, with a pot of coffee steaming on the top. The main feature of the dusty but warm little room was a massive roll-top desk, the kind with many little drawers. Stacks of papers were piled everywhere, all covered with a fine dust from the mill.

On summer days, while we waited our turn, we walked to the dam to look for trout that we could often spot lurking in the cool, clear water. Or sometimes we checked the miller's fishing pole, to see if the bobber was still floating. If we were thirsty we walked to the other side of the mill, where water poured from a pipe. Pa said it was from a spring and we could get a drink there anytime, the best tasting fresh water we'd ever find.

When it was our turn, Pa dragged our gunny bags to the little square holes in the mill's floor and dumped them. From the days when I was a toddler, Pa always warned me to stand back when he was dumping the sacks. "Wouldn't want you falling into the mill." The mill floor was highly polished and slippery from the thousands of gunnysacks that had been dragged across it.

I could hear the grain tumble down the metal chute to the grinding mechanism in the basement near where the water turbine turned and powered the mill. The mill, through a series of belts with little buckets on them, carried the ground feed to the upper reaches of the building, where it was dumped into sacking chutes. It wasn't long before our ground grist appeared at a chute to which we attached our empty bags for filling.

The grist tumbling into our open sacks was warm and sweet-smelling. When our bags of ground grist were filled, we dragged them across the slippery floor to a scale where the miller weighed them and recorded the weights on a slip of paper. We paid a few cents a pound for the grinding and loaded our gunny bags of warm grist in the back of the Plymouth and started home. In two weeks we would return, repeating what we had just done.

History of Gristmills

Old gristmills are reminders of settlement days. A community began with a flour mill, a general store, a tavern, a church, and a school. In much of the Midwest, pioneer farmers grew wheat and the first mills ground wheat into flour. This continued until the 1870s, when wheat growing became difficult and some farmers switched to dairy farming. As farmers grew less wheat, the mills quit grinding flour and began grinding grist for cows. As dairy farming changed and the number of dairy farmers declined, the small water-powered mills closed. A few of the mills turned from water to electrical power, became larger, and ground tons of cattle feed. But most of them closed. Some former gristmills have become museums, antique stores, craft shops, and homes. More have been forgotten—abandoned buildings sitting alongside millponds.

Country Stores

Country stores came in various sizes and shapes; some were located at the crossroads in a rural neighborhood, near a church, or a country tavern. Many were found in villages, clustered among other businesses such as hardware stores, barbershops, and doctor's offices. Today a few remain, here and there, reminders of an earlier time, before computer cash registers and self-serve supermarkets.

Ma always shopped at the Mercantile Store on Saturday night. I often tagged along because the Mercantile was one of the most interesting places in our rural community.

At the Mercantile, Ma traded her eggs for groceries; sometimes she got money back; occasionally she had to pay a little more.

Arnol Roberts, a slightly-built man, and his equally slightly-built wife, owned and operated the Mercantile, a two-story brick building with multiple purposes. The upstairs was a dance hall where people danced the polka at wedding receptions, birthday parties, or anniversaries. One Saturday night customers on the first floor noticed that the ceiling light fixtures were swaying to the music. A state inspector came by, and there were no more dances.

Next to the dance floor was a dentist's office, reached by climbing an open iron fire escape. Everything was painful about the visit to the dentist, including the long, scary climb to his office.

Two bowling lanes were located in the basement, not used since the bowling alley next door was built. But for me, the most important feature of the basement was the collection of books found there. Mr. Roberts often led me to the basement to see the books. He knew I was interested in reading and that I had few books at home. What wonderful books they were: *Treasure Island, Swiss Family Robinson, Little Men, Little Women, The Black Arrow, Alice's Adventures in Wonderland.* Each was in hardcover, and each sold for forty-nine cents. I saved my money and every month or so paged through this wonderful collection and listened to Mr. Roberts' recommendation about which one I should buy.

The first floor of the Mercantile had a clothing department with racks of barn coats, OshKosh B' Gosh overalls, flannel shirts for winter, thin cotton shirts for summer, straw hats, and winter caps—the best ones with cat-fur earflaps.

On the wall to the left, boxes of shoes were stacked higher than even Arnol Roberts could reach. They were mostly work shoes, with tops that came above the ankle. Scattered among the rows of work shoes were a few low-top shoes, the kind people wore to church, to weddings and funerals, and to polka dances. Rubber boots were stacked next to the shoes, the smell of new rubber almost overpowering the smell of new leather. A person could buy a two-buckle boot, a four-buckle boot, and, best of all, a six-buckle boot. The more buckles, the higher the boot and the deeper the barnyard muck that could be waded through without getting wet feet.

Next to the rubber boots were the barn rubbers, the kind I wore when I went for the cows on a dewy morning. Here and there, stacked on shelves and piled on the top of everything else, were children's toys—dolls, teddy bears, wagons, sleds, card games, and checkerboards. Around Christmastime Mr. Roberts brought the toys together, sort of, so that shoppers didn't need to look all around the store for the toy they wanted.

The dry goods department was on the wall opposite the shoes. Piled on shelves were bolts of cloth that Mrs. Roberts unrolled for Ma so she could decide on material for a dress or shirts for my brothers or an apron for Aunt Minnie, whose birthday was coming up. With the decision made, Mrs. Roberts tore off the proper length of cloth, neatly folded it, wrapped it in brown paper, and strung a length of white string around it in both directions.

The grocery department was on the end of the store. Ma always came with a grocery list that she handed to Arnol or his wife, who went looking for what she wanted and brought it back to the counter. The groceries were stacked in Ma's egg crate.

Back of the grocery counter were stacks of cornflakes

and oatmeal boxes, cans of pork and beans, tomato soup, tins of sardines, canned red salmon from some far-off place I had never heard of, and more. At the meat counter one could buy anything from pork chops to beef steak, but Ma never bought any meat—we had our own at home.

Outside of the books in the basement, the best thing at the Mercantile was the ice-cream cooler. Open the round lid, and here were metal tubs of ice cream—vanilla, strawberry, and chocolate. For five cents, I could buy a double-dip ice-cream cone. In summer Dad often asked Mr. Roberts to dip out a half-gallon of ice cream that we ate around the kitchen table when we got home. It was our once a week treat because our icebox was never cold enough to keep ice cream.

History of Country Stores

Country stores served many purposes. Most sold groceries and basic clothing items; some also had gasoline pumps. Occasionally a country store sold cattle feed, agricultural seeds, fish bait, hardware, and beer. Most had a table and a few chairs in a corner available for playing checkers or drinking a cup of coffee.

County stores were sometimes Greyhound bus stops, with a bench outside for bus riders to rest and wait. Before Rural Free Delivery, farmers picked up their mail at the local post office in the country store.

Country stores also served as social centers. Women learned from other women what was going on in the community—who was sick, who had traveled somewhere, who had done something that caused tongues to wag. Men talked about the weather, crops, cows, the cost of a new plow, or the cheese factory price for milk.

With automobiles and improved roads, many local shoppers passed by the country store on their way to bigger and fancier stores in the cities.

Barbershops

Nearly every small town had a barbershop. Many were established when the community was first settled, so visiting one today is like seeing a piece of local history. Customers shared the news, told stories, found out where the fish were biting—and some customers even had their hair cut.

Ma cut my hair with a hand-operated clipper that pulled like the dickens. Getting a haircut was in the same category as having a tooth drilled. When she finished with her hair-pulling clippers, loose hair was settled between my long underwear and my skin, and I itched until Saturday night, which was bath night.

On special occasions, Pa took me to the barber in town. This was usually just before the school Christmas program and one or two other times during the year. Mr. Ehlert was the barber, a man of considerable reputation for his ability to talk nonstop.

The barbershop was in a little room behind the bank and right on the shore of the millpond. From the barbershop window a person could see the water and sometimes spot a trout swimming there.

One cold day in mid-December, Pa dropped me off at the barbershop and said he'd come back in about an hour to pick me up. I soon learned that I'd be second, so I picked up a copy of *Outdoor Life* and began paging through it. What I really wanted was to hear some barbershop stories. But I suspect that because I was a kid, the men laid off on the good stuff that I really wanted to hear.

Nothing seemed to quiet Mr. Ehlert. He went on about the weather, about the millpond just freezing over, about how mean the winter was likely to be, and about the trouble Emil Sorenson was having with his horses. One topic to another, without a break, or even scarcely taking a breath. The electric clipper hummed, the shears clicked, and a pile of hair accumulated on the floor.

Soon the customer was finished, got up from the chair, and looked at himself in the mirror before putting on his cap and coat.

"Next," said Mr. Ehlert.

I crawled up in the chair and made myself comfortable.

"You're Herman Apps' kid, aren't you?"

"I am."

"How do want your hair cut?"

"So it looks good for the Christmas program," I answered.

"And it will," said Mr. Ehlert as he grabbed his clippers and began buzzing around my ears. Mr. Ehlert kept on talking nonstop, but I didn't listen much. I was thinking about Christmas and whether I'd be getting some new skis this year.

When he finished, he asked, "Want some smelly stuff on your neck?"

"Sure...sure," I replied. I hadn't been listening.

Soon Mr. Ehlert was rubbing lilac-smelling water on my neck. It smelled a little strong.

Pa hadn't come back yet, so I sat down in an empty chair to wait.

"Next," Mr. Ehlert said.

He took the barber cloth and gave it a massive shake so that it snapped.

A big, burly-looking man stood up. He was huge, well over six feet tall and wide as an oak tree. I didn't know him and couldn't recall that I'd ever seen him.

He shuffled across the floor and sat down heavily in the barber chair. Mr. Ehlert flung the barber cloth around the man's neck, fastening it in the back.

"And how would you like your hair cut?"

"In silence, please."

Well, you'd think that a tree had fallen on Mr. Ehlert. He turned an odd shade of white, and for a moment he said nothing. The other men in the barbershop heard the exchange and began laughing, louder and louder.

Mr. Ehlert pretended he didn't hear them as he busied himself cutting the hair of this customer who requested silence. Folks later said that Mr. Ehlert was quieter that day than they had ever remembered. Just then Pa came by and we left. I couldn't wait to tell him what I had just witnessed.

History of Barbershops

Similar to the country tavern, gristmill, and country store, men gathered (they still do) at barbershops to share news, tell stories, and have their hair trimmed, usually in that order.

Bernard Zelinske, an 81-year-old barber in Redgranite, Wisconsin, has worked in a barbershop since he was a youngster. His father, who had come from Poland, was a barber before him. Zelinske got his start shining shoes at the shoeshine stand in a corner of his father's shop. "Saturday night was the night for shoeshines," Zelinske recalled. "I got a nickel for a shine in the early 1930s, and with two nickels I could see a show."

Soon young Zelinske graduated to more important tasks such as helping with shaving. "I would lather up, and Dad did the shaving. I'd finish the job by shaving guys' necks, and then they were out the door. I did a lot of soaping and lathering. Guys would come in twice a week to get a shave. We got 20 cents for each one."

By the time Zelinske was 17, he knew how to cut hair and was helping in the shop. He spent some time in a Civilian Conservation Corps (CCC) camp near St. Croix Falls, where he cut hair. In 1941 he was drafted into the army, and he continued to cut hair. He was back home in December 1945 and began his official barber apprenticeship in 1946, at the age of 28. Of course, by this time, he had unofficially cut hair for many years.

"My barbershop's hours were 8:00 to 6:00 during the week, Wednesday nights until 10:00, and Saturday nights until 10:00," Zelinske said. "Saturday night was the big night for a shave and a hair-cut. A lot of times we wouldn't get out of here until 11:00. There was a dance every Saturday night, and lot of the guys would go from the barbershop to the dance. I'd powder them and put smelly stuff on their face, and they were off dancing."

Zelinske had a checkerboard on a table in the corner of the barbershop. Especially during the Depression years, men would come into his shop to play checkers and "shoot the breeze," even if they didn't need a haircut. "There wasn't much work then, and they'd come in here rather than go to the tavern," Zelenske said.

Don Apps, the author's brother, started cutting hair in Oshkosh in 1957, moved to Sheboygan, where he owned and managed a barbershop until 1982, and then cut hair part-time in Princeton, Wisconsin, for several years.

He remembers that one of his customers didn't come in for a long time, then one day sat down in his chair for a haircut. "I'm cutting his hair, and we're talking," Don related. "All of a sudden, I quit talking because I'm working on the left side of his head and I pull his ear down a little to get the hair off and the ear starts coming loose. I'm thinking, oh, my God! There must be something wrong with this ear; it was kind of cold. But how am I gonna tell this guy that his ear is coming off? Then I look around at the other customers—are they seeing this guy's ear is starting to fall off? I start looking for blood, but there's no blood. I'm really starting to sweat by now. Finally, the guy says, 'Is my ear coming off?'"

"Yeah," I says.

"Had surgery a while back, and I guess I didn't glue my new ear on very well this morning."

Fritz, a barber in Don's shop, sometimes pulled a trick on customers who wore glasses. While cutting a customer's hair, Fritz would place the customer's glasses on the back bar. When Fritz finished a haircut, he'd take another broken pair he'd put aside and switch them with the customer's real glasses. Just before he put the broken pair on the person's head, he'd drop them on the floor and the lens would fall out. "Oh, sorry," Fritz would say when he handed the glasses without the lens to the customer. "The guy was usually madder than hell," Don related.

Like taverns and country stores, barbershops were community institutions that were there for a specific purpose but served many other needs as well.

4-H Clubs

A four-leaf clover with an H on each leaf is the symbol for 4-H, an organization designed for farm boys and girls so that they could have fun, learn to work together, and gain information about modern farming and homemaking. The 4-H motto, "To Make the Best Better," and the organization's emphasis on Head, Hands, Heart, and Health (what the "H"s stand for) have been a guide for rural children since the early 1900s.

Pa said one night at the supper table, "We ought to get a 4-H club going in this community."

I was old enough to belong, and in a couple years my brothers could join, too.

At the Courthouse, Pa talked to the County Agent, who agreed to come to the Chain O' Lake school and tell us what 4-H was all about and what we needed to do to start a club. The county agent said we should invite the neighborhood kids who were ten and older to come to the meeting. I asked the Dudley girls, the Kolka boys, Clair Jenks, Mildred Swen, and the York boys to come.

We all gathered at the schoolhouse one Monday evening. The county agent, a pleasant, soft-spoken man with a round face, told us about 4-H and how to organize a club. "You need at least a half-dozen kids," he said.

He explained that we'd enroll in one of several projects: calf, cooking, clothing, forestry, woodworking, or a field crop project. Once we signed up, we'd get government bulletins that explained what to do and how to keep a record of our work.

It sounded mighty interesting, especially when he explained that we could take our projects to the fair.

Going to the fair was what everyone in the room wanted to do.

I listened to the county agent explain that 4-H clubs were democratic organizations—the kids voted on what they wanted to do. That sounded good to me. I knew that at home if I came up with an idea Pa or Ma didn't like, it didn't go anywhere.

"What do we do first?" I asked.

"Decide on a name for your club," the county agent said.

"*Hard workers*," one of the Dudley girls offered.

"Dumb name," a York boy blurted out.

"Every suggestion should have a chance," the county agent said as he wrote Hard Workers on the blackboard.

"How about *Chain O' Lake*, after our school," Mildred S. offered.

"Boring," said the other York boy.

Jim Kolka then stood up. "I think we should call our club the *Royal Dizzy Daisies*. It's a special name."

"I like it," said the York boys in unison.

The county agent, with all three names displayed on the blackboard, pointed to each name and asked for a show of hands.

Royal Dizzy Daisies won with a vast margin. What a name, I thought, and we had done it ourselves. Democracy was great. Then I heard a buzz in the back of the schoolroom, where the parents were listening in.

Mrs. Dudley had her hand up. "You sure you want *Royal Dizzy Daisies* for your name?" she asked.

Mrs. Jenks asked the question a little differently. "If you name the 4-H club the same as the school, then people would know where to find it."

Before you could say *democracy*, the name had been changed to *Chain O' Lake 4-H* club. So much for kids making their own decisions, I thought.

We all gained a lot from 4-H, including learning that decisions made democratically were sometimes subject to higher review.

History of 4-H Clubs

In the late 1800s, 4-H clubs began as corn clubs for boys and canning clubs for girls. By 1900 several rural leaders had concluded that farm boys and girls were not learning enough about farming in the rural schools, and they encouraged county school superintendents to organize boys' and girls' clubs.

Some boys' and girls' clubs began using a three-leaf clover with three Hs. Later the fourth H, Health, was added. These clubs had no formal tie to any governmental agency. This changed when Congress passed the Smith-Lever Act in 1914, creating the Cooperative Extension Service within the United States Department of Agriculture. Cooperative Extension was formed as a cooperative arrangement between the national government (USDA), the state land grant universities, and county government. The Smith-Lever law provided for the hiring of county extension agents, soon found in nearly every county in the United States. Besides working with farmers and their wives, these agents also organized 4-H clubs.

Through the county extension office, 4-H members had access to the latest agricultural research from the agricultural colleges ranging from crop and livestock raising to preserving food and caring for rural health needs.

Laverne Forest, now an orchard owner, was a 4-H member in Minnesota. He said, "What I did in 4-H got me started in what I'm doing now. It was a chance for us rural kids, isolated as we were, to belong to something, to play softball, and take stuff to the county fair. We had our 4-H club meetings at the Asbury one-room country school. We had a chance to be president of the 4-H club, and that was really something. I was into tractors, mechanics, and shop. I fixed machinery, built wagons and corn cribs. I put the whole plumbing system in on our farm. I also raised raspberries and helped Dad plant apple trees. In 1950 our family was growing a half to an acre of raspberries. I picked them, got a nickel a pint, and thought I was rich."

Lavern Forest's story is not different from those of thousands of farm children who belonged to 4-H clubs.

In recent years 4-H clubs have also become available to village and urban young people. Though considerably different from the days of corn and canning clubs, 4-H continues to flourish and provide informal educational opportunities for thousands of young people.

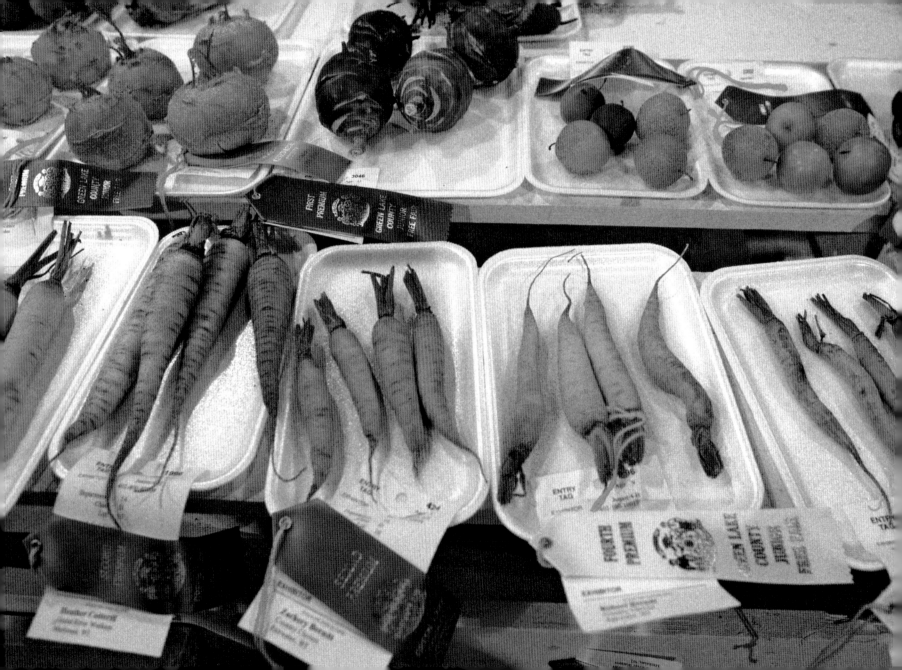

County Fairs

County fairs are Ferris wheels and merry-go-rounds, fried onions and cotton candy, 4-H clubs, and Future Farmers of America. They are prizewinning bread, first-place carrots, and grand-champion Holsteins. They are strength-testing machines (ring the bell with a mallet), dart-throwing games (break three balloons and win a stuffed animal), and dunk machines (dump the clown in the water tank with a well-aimed throw). They are as old as America and older.

*I*t was my first year to sleep over at the county fair. I was caring for my 4-H calf and excited beyond belief. Several other boys from our 4-H club were also staying over; we all slept in the loft above the cattle.

Word had gotten around that an airplane was coming to the fair. The only airplanes I had seen were those flying high over our farm. Now maybe I could see one up close. I saw a sign with a picture of a plane nailed on the side of the cattle barn. "See your farm from the air," the sign said. "$5.00 for fifteen minutes."

How I wished I could ride in a plane, but five dollars was far more than I could afford. I had just enough money to buy three meals a day at the fairgrounds, nothing extra for an airplane ride.

We had just settled our 4-H calves in their stalls, spread out fresh straw, and piled alfalfa hay in the mangers, when I heard a roar that I knew must be the airplane. I looked out the barn door and sure enough, a giant two-wing airplane was skimming low over the trees east of the fairgrounds, just beyond the racetrack. An area had been cleared in an open field, a makeshift landing strip with rows of trees on each end and a wire fence all around—it must have been somebody's cow pasture.

What a sight it was. The pilot had throttled back on the engine, and I heard wind whistling through the propeller. I could see the pilot. He sat in a cutout place toward the back of the bright red plane, above the two wings. He wore a leather cap with big smoky-colored goggles over his eyes. One end of a long white scarf, which was wrapped around his neck, bellowed out in the wind like the tail of a kite.

Closer and closer the plane came to the trees, dropping out of the sky, gently touching the ground, and then roaring across the grassy field. The pasture wasn't all that smooth as I could see the plane bouncing along, the wings tipping up and down. The pilot revved the engine, turned the big red machine around, and headed toward the wire fence where my fellow 4-H members and I were watching. The plane stopped just short of the fence. The pilot cut the engine, climbed out on a wing, and dropped to the ground.

He was a youngish, tall fellow with especially long legs. He pulled off his leather-goggled helmet and walked over to where we stood, our mouths hanging open and our eyes wide with excitement.

"Anybody here want a ride?" he asked. "A chance to see your house from the air?"

An older fellow held up his hand and said he wanted a ride. He pulled a five-dollar bill from his billfold and handed it to the pilot.

The pilot helped him into the passenger compartment and yanked on the propeller. The engine coughed, caught, and the propeller began spinning. Soon the red flying machine was taxiing toward the far end of the pasture.

With an ear-shattering roar, the plane raced across the uneven field and lifted into the air, a picture of grace and beauty. It banked, flew over us, and headed west, soon disappearing from view. We decided to wait for its return, exchanging comments about what we had just seen and the wonder of it. Soon we heard the engine and saw the bi-winger come into view, lining up to land as it had before.

None of us saw what the pilot did wrong. The wheels of the plane must have caught the wire fence because rather than bump along the field, one wing struck the ground and broke and the nose dug in, smashing the propeller. When the dust cleared, the pilot crawled from the wreck holding his arm. His passenger also crawled out, blood streaming down his face from a cut on his forehead.

My fellow 4-H members and I commented on how fortunate we were to not have enough money for a plane ride. Whoever had ridden in the plane would have missed showing his calf in the ring the next day for sure.

History of County Fairs

County fairs began in Europe, especially England, where gentlemen farmers displayed their livestock at community events. During Colonial years in the United States, farmers organized agricultural societies, the first in 1784. By 1860, 941 agricultural societies were operating in the United States with the primary purpose of encouraging improvement in agriculture. In 1811 the Berkshire Agricultural Society of Massachusetts organized a competitive display for farmers, including cash prizes for livestock. By the 1850s fairs were operating in the Midwest.

Today about 3,500 fairs are held each year in the United States and Canada (about 800 in Canada). Illinois holds about 105 fairs each year, Wisconsin 100, and Minnesota 95.

County fairs are show places for adults and youth, especially 4-H and FFA members who exhibit their projects. Fairs bring people together to have fun, to compete with each other, to enjoy time away from hard work and regular responsibilities. A day at the fair, from the youngest member of a family to the oldest, is always one to remember.

Town Halls

In a time when much is said about state and national government, town halls remind us of government that is close to the people, when folks know their local governmental officials because they are their neighbors and their friends.

An old town hall looks like a one-room country school without the bell tower. Many town halls had but one room, with a few chairs and tables. It isn't the building that was important, for these were and many still are insignificant structures. The importance of the town hall was that it represented the smallest unit of government in many states.

I had ridden by our town hall many times. Pa had pointed it out and told me that important things happened there. "It's where we can have our say," Pa said. I didn't know what he meant and couldn't figure out how having your say had anything to do with this rather rickety little building sitting near a millpond.

At breakfast one November morning in 1944, Pa announced that it was election day and that when I got home from school, I should come along with Ma and him to the town hall where the voting took place.

"Voting is something you should see," Pa said.

I wasn't too enthused in tagging along to see people vote—I really didn't know how they did it, but it didn't seem the least bit interesting.

"Today we vote for town chairman, and we also vote for President of the United States. We have our say in who will run our township and who will run our country," Pa said.

Pa was waiting when I got home from school, and with Ma we headed off to the town hall some four miles from our farm.

I knew something about the election; we had talked about it in school, and I'd heard Pa talking with other farmers about the candidates when we waited for our grist at the mill. Nobody talked much about the town chairman race. Hard to talk for or against a neighbor. But the presidential race was something else.

One day I overhead Pa proclaiming the virtues of Franklin Roosevelt, who was running for a third term. "Can't argue that Roosevelt got us out of the Depression," Pa said.

"Yeah, if the war hadn't started, we'd still have Depression," another farmer said. He had loudly

announced that he was voting for Republican Tom Dewey from New York.

I'd overheard these discussions, but the names ran in one ear and right out the other.

At the town hall, Pa and Ma greeted people as they entered the rather plainly furnished building. There was a big box on a table into which a woman was stuffing folded sheets of paper as people handed them to her.

I expected to hear talk about the candidates, but there was no mention of the election and what was going on. People were lining up to get their ballots, marking them, and handing them to the woman at the big box.

That day I learned a little about voting as a way to have your say and how important Pa, Ma, and our neighbors believed it to be. I also discovered a little more about the importance of this plain little, poorly furnished building called a town hall.

History of Town Halls

Town government, which began in 1636 in Providence, Rhode Island, is the oldest existing form of government still continuing in the United States. When the Declaration of Independence was signed in 1776, 38 of the 56 signers came from states with town government. Today town government is found in only 20 states, including several in the Midwest: Illinois, Indiana, Michigan, Minnesota, Ohio, and Wisconsin. Town government is also found in New England and in New York, New Jersey, and Pennsylvania.

What makes town government special is the town meeting, an annual opportunity for town residents to talk with their elected officials about such matters as taxes, roads, and other local concerns. Town government is operated by three to seven elected officials, depending on the state and the population of the town.

The responsibilities of town government include maintaining town roads (including plowing and mowing), providing a polling place for local, state, and national elections, assessing and collecting property taxes (most of the money collected goes to other governmental units), maintaining bridges, passing and enforcing certain local ordinances such as those related to land use, and issuing building permits. Some towns are also responsible for fire and police protection.

Towns also occasionally do creative things. For instance, in the Town of Springwater, Waushara County, Wisconsin, local residents built a wooden covered bridge across the Pine River near the village of Saxeville. A 70-year-old concrete bridge had been condemned. The town was slated to receive federal and state aid to construct a steel and concrete bridge that would cost about $150,000. Supervisor Garth Towne had seen several covered bridges in Pennsylvania and thought such a bridge would add a nice touch to the Springwater community. With the leadership of Mr. Towne and town chairman Everett Eckstein, volunteers were enlisted to build the bridge. Work began in July 1996, and the bridge was completed in time for a June 1, 1997, dedication. Total cost of the very attractive wooden bridge was $50,000. No state or federal tax dollars were involved.

One-Room Country Schools

Nearly all one-room country schools are now closed, but many of the buildings remain, as do the memories for those who attended them and went on to become farmers, teachers and nurses, professors and attorneys, carpenters and electricians, deans and mayors. The one-room country school is clearly a symbol of rural education in much of the United States.

Mrs. Faith Jenks said it often in those days before the Christmas program, when we were practicing our pieces, learning our lines in the skits, and trying to stay in tune during the songs.

"Remember," she said. She only had to raise her voice the least little bit, and everyone in our country school stopped what we were doing and listened. "When we do the nativity scene, there will be no giggling, no snickering, no poking each other, no whispering. No nothing. Do you all understand?"

"Yes, Mrs. Jenks," we said in unison.

And so it came to pass. The night of the annual Christmas program arrived, that dreaded but wonderful night when we got to wear new bib overalls, new shirts, and sometimes even new shoes. That night when we stood on a rickety plank stage nailed to wooden sawhorses and performed for our parents, our brothers and sisters, our aunts, uncles and cousins, our neighbors, everyone who lived in the community. Everyone.

The program was going well. People laughed at the right places. They clapped after each performance, loud and long. But now it was time for the nativity scene. That most important event. That part of the program when Mary walked onstage, wearing a bedsheet tied around her head. And Joseph, with a bathrobe he'd borrowed that was too long, walked beside her.

Keep from smiling, I reminded myself. For heaven's sake keep from giggling. This is serious business. No matter that Frank Wilton looked dumb as Joseph. Worse than dumb.

Mary and Joseph knelt by the sawbuck filled with straw and containing the baby Jesus, some girl's naked doll.

Don't even smirk. Nothing funny here. Nothing. Not unless Frank trips on his bathrobe.

Mrs. Jenks took her place at the old brown upright piano that stood against the wall. To play the instrument, she had her back to the stage and to the front row made up of students.

For a moment, a great quiet came over the room. Not a whisper from anyone in the audience. Respect for the nativity scene.

Then Mrs. Jenks began to play "Away in the Manger" and a trio of three of our best vocalists began singing the words. "Away in the manger, no crib for his bed."

A touching scene. Done with feeling. Performed with reverence. And then it happened. We all knew that mice had, earlier in the fall, built a nest in the piano, but we thought we had trapped all of them. Obviously not.

A shy little field mouse, awakened by the clatter of piano hammers pounding against wires, stuck his head out the top of the piano, in a place Mrs. Jenks could not see.

"The little Lord Jesus lay down his sweet head," the choir continued.

I saw the mouse first and poked Jim, who was sitting next to me. He immediately burst out laughing. I could see the color on the back of Mrs. Jenks' neck turn red.

The mouse crawled down the piano, then paraded across the stage, stopping dead center, only a few feet from where baby Jesus lay asleep in the hay. All the kids in the front row were giggling. Mrs. Jenks' neck grew redder. Then folks in the back of the room saw the mouse and began laughing, loud laughing. Knee-pounding laughing. Mrs. Jenks, furious by now, wheeled around, ready to chastise everyone in the schoolroom. Then she saw the mouse, too, and a slow smile spread across her face.

A school board member with a broom encouraged the mouse off the stage, and after a few fretful moments and some isolated shrieks, the mouse ran out the door. The school program continued. Mary readjusted her sheet. Joseph tightened the rope around his waist, and Mrs. Jenks took her place on the piano bench. Not a smile was seen, not even a smirk.

History of One-Room Country Schools

When settlers arrived in an area, one of the first things they did was build a school, a one-room building where all eight grades met together with one teacher. For many years these schools, located about four miles apart, had no electricity, central heating, indoor plumbing, telephone, or lunch program. The teachers—most of them women—began teaching with only one or two years of training beyond high school. Many were not yet 20 years old when they started teaching at a country school.

Reading, writing, and arithmetic—the three Rs—were heavily emphasized, but so was spelling and geography, history and science, even art and music.

Students had at least four opportunities to master a subject—when they discussed it during recitation, when they heard the class ahead of them discuss it, when they heard the class behind them discuss it, and when they tried to help a slower student understand it. As the teacher had many students to teach and all eight grades to cover, students learned to help themselves and to help each other.

Not only were the one-room schools places for learning, they also served as community gathering places. Country schools provided an identity for rural communities. People referred to where they lived by the name of their school. When they closed and the children were bused to the nearby village schools, much more was lost than merely a country school.

Country Churches

For years, country churches have been an important part of rural communities. They are reminders of church picnics, Sunday school programs, and Ladies' Aid meetings. They are a powerful symbol of rural people who believed in themselves, believed in their neighbors and communities, and above all, believed in a Higher Power.

I expected the worst when I overhead Ma mention my name while talking with Reverend Renner one morning after church. What had I done that was so terrible that it required a conversation with the preacher? As it turned out, it wasn't so much what I had done but what I would be doing.

Pa got in on it, too. For several years I had wanted a bicycle, but Pa said I had two good legs and should use them. Then one day, out of the blue, he said he'd heard about a bike for sale and wondered if I wanted to have a look at it. I'd saved up my potato-picking money for a bicy-

cle, and now it looked as if I'd have a chance to spend it.

The fellow selling the bike said it was only five years old, was in good condition, and was just the thing for a kid like me. It had shiny silver fenders, front and back, a slightly worn leather seat, and a wire basket fastened to the handlebars. It was the most wonderful bicycle I had ever seen, and I quickly agreed to buy it, with Pa nodding his head in agreement.

At the time, I saw no connection between Ma's conversation with the preacher and my new bike. I soon found out that Ma and Pa had decided that I was destined to spend every morning all summer learning catechism at the Lutheran church. My new bike was how I would travel the nearly five miles to get there.

I figured that I could invest a few summer mornings sitting around listening to Reverend Renner in return for a bike. Besides, I'd be avoiding a lot of farmwork on those mornings when I was learning profound things about the church and its beliefs.

I discovered that five more kids were destined to suffer through the same summer morning fate. When I first saw them, I wondered how many of them got bikes or something else in trade for showing up every day with a sharp pencil and an open mind.

"Welcome," said Reverend Renner that first Monday morning. He was a tall, thin man with high cheekbones. This was the first time I had seen him without his robes. Surprisingly, he looked a whole lot like an ordinary man. I always thought he must be right close to God, but without his robes he looked like he might be a leap or two away.

He started right out. "What is the source book for all Christian doctrine?" I glanced over at Emil sitting next to me. I could see he didn't know. I surely didn't. I didn't even know what source book meant.

As was the case all summer, little "do everything right when you're in church" Linda thrust up her hand.

"Yes, Linda."

"The source book for all Christian doctrine is the Holy Bible," she answered in a know-it-all voice that caused me to cringe. I could see a long summer coming up, a very heavy payment for my bike with the silver fenders.

"How many books in the Bible?" Reverend Renner asked. He looked right at me.

"A bunch," I said. "Lots of em."

"There are sixty-six," Reverend Renner said without so much as a smile. "And here's how you can remember. You have your Old Testament and your New Testament. Three letters in the word old, nine letters in testament. Three and nine next to each other become thirty-nine. Three letters in new, nine letters in testament. Three times nine is twenty-seven. Add twenty-seven and thirty-nine and you get what?"

Quickly I scratched down the two numbers and added them. "Sixty-six," I answered.

"Correct. See how easy it is."

But it wasn't easy and his fancy method didn't help. I wrote down sixty-six, and next to the numbers, Phillips 66. When he asked me the question again, I'd think about gasoline and remember—I hoped.

So the summer went. Each morning I hopped on my bike, pedaled the sandy road that went by our farm, got on blacktop County A, and pushed on toward the church, trying to sneak by the two or three farms where dogs chased me.

Each morning I sat through another episode of Linda's showing off her vast knowledge of the Bible and all things Lutheran. My bike was costing me more each day as I tried to soak up the thousands of facts that I absolutely needed to know—according to Reverend Renner.

Then it was over. I pedaled my bike into the yard for the last time. No more catechism tomorrow. I noticed the last couple of days that the bike wasn't going just right. So today, this final day of riding to church, I decided to make some adjustments. I took off the front wheel, and all the bearings fell out in my hand. Not only had catechism worn me out, it had worn out my bike. I couldn't ride it again until I saved enough money to buy new wheel bearings. I prayed that wouldn't be long.

History of Country Churches

Rural churches are of many types. In the Midwest, large numbers of Lutheran churches were built by Scandinavian and German settlers—different kinds of churches for different groups. However, Methodist, Presbyterian, Baptist, and Catholic churches were also readily founded.

Some of the earliest churches in the region were constructed by Catholic missionaries working in the area. For instance, Father Samuel Mazzuchelli arrived in what was to become Wisconsin in 1835. He located near the Mississippi River in a region populated with lead miners, and he began building churches. Between 1835 and his death in 1864, Father Mazzuchelli built 24 Catholic churches. Most of them are gone today. But a few remain; one

141

stands in New Diggings, Wisconsin. This church, St. Augustine's, was built in 1844 and closed in 1925. At one time the congregation had 120 members.

Several unusual church congregations formed in some rural communities. Near Wild Rose, Wisconsin, a congregation of Freethinkers formed the Standalone Church. They had no definite creed or dogma, no pastor; everyone believed as he wanted. Thus the title for the congregation—Standalone. The thread that tied them together was a belief in God.

One of the reasons many immigrants migrated to the United States was religious freedom—the opportunity to worship God as one wished. Immigrants expressed religious freedom in a variety of ways, in an assortment of church congregations that sprang up throughout the region. Many of these church buildings stand today with active congregations that have been in existence well over 100 years.

Farm Auctions

Farm auctions have been held as long as farmers have worked the land and then found it necessary to sell and move on. Auctions are symbols of change, sometimes signaling defeat, other times chronicling the end of a long, successful career. In every instance, auctions evoke memories.

When Grandpa Witt died, Pa was put in charge of settling things up. "First thing we gotta do is hold an auction," he said.

On a cold blustery day in April, everyone gathered at the Witt farm. Promptly at 10:00, the auctioneer, a plump, middle-aged man wearing a cowboy hat, announced that the auction was beginning.

A steel-wheeled hay wagon had been pushed in front of the pump house. The wagon was piled high with forks, milk cans, hammers, saws, garden hoes, used water pipes, wrenches, buckets of bolts and nails—things that accu-

mulate on a farm. The auctioneer grabbed a shovel and began: "What am I offered for this good shovel? Who wants to start it off? Do I hear five dollars, anybody give me a five dollar bill for this good shovel?"

He had a patter, a singsong way of stringing words together that made people listen, that sometimes excited people and made them bid higher than they intended.

"Anybody give me a dollar," the auctioneer chanted. "Got a dollar and now two. Who'll give me two, and three, and four?" The bidding picked up and then as rapidly stopped. Farmers knew the cost of a new shovel at

the hardware store, and they weren't going to pay more for a used one, most of the time anyway.

"All done, I'm gonna sell it." Brief pause. "Sold, to that fellow with the red cap, and mark it cheap."

About half the time, the auctioneer said, "Mark it cheap." He wanted people to believe, no matter what they paid, that they got a bargain. Pa and I stood in the background, at the edge of the crowd, watching.

The auction continued, items large and small—a McCormick grain binder, a corn binder, chicken feeders, a hay loader and a side-delivery rake, a one-bottom plow and a two-row corn planter, a disc and a grain drill with grass seed attachment, a spike-tooth drag. Implements for farming.

"Got a good team of horses here," the auctioneer intoned. An assistant had harnessed them and driven them in front of the crowd. "We're selling them with the harnesses, so you get the whole package."

The pair of gray horses fidgeted and tossed their heads in the air. They were not accustomed to crowds.

"Stand back," the auctioneer instructed. "We'll drive them a little, show you that they're in good shape and got good feet."

The assistant drove the team toward the road and brought them back at a trot, yelling "Whoa!" when they were once more in front of the auctioneer.

"What am I bid for this team of good horses?" the auctioneer began.

Pa nudged me and whispered, "It's a willing team."

"What?" I whispered back.

"One horse is willing to pull and the other is willing to let him."

"Oh," I said, smiling. I knew the buyer would find out soon enough what kind of team he'd purchased.

Late in the afternoon the auctioneer turned to the household goods—a wringer washing machine, a hand meat grinder, pots and pans, beds, bureaus, and an oak secretary. There was more. A wood box, a small round wood stove, wicker planters, a wooden bed, picture frames, and sadirons.

And then the last items were sold and the crowd drifted off, people carrying what they had purchased. Pa and I went into the house. Ma was sitting with Grandma Witt at the kitchen table. Grandma, a thin little woman with white hair, was crying. I hadn't seen her cry before.

History of Farm Auctions

 Farm auctions are held because of a death or often because of injury or illness: the farmer loses an arm in a corn picker or suffers a heart attack, and the family cannot continue. Sometimes the medical bills have piled so high that the auction is necessary to pay them.

Too often, auctions result when farm debts exceed farm income and the feed dealer, the implement store manager, and the local banker come knocking, come looking for their money. The money is not available, for the price of milk has been low, a drought has ruined the corn and soybean crop, or a hundred other calamities have befallen the farm family. The only solution is an auction, selling off the cows and the tractors, selling the plows and the wagons, selling everything that is needed to make money because not enough money was made.

Some farm auctions are conducted under less difficult circumstances. The farmer is retiring and moving to town, doing what farmers in communities have done for years. No matter what the reason, a farm auction is a difficult time for those selling.

PART V: RESTING AND PLAYING

Little Red Wagons

Many kids, including those from the farm, grew up with red wagons. They used them to tote a favorite toy, haul wood from the woodpile to the woodshed, and lug around (when they were forced to) their baby brothers and sisters. Children imagined the wagons were steam locomotives and fancy automobiles. Kids rode them down steep hills and pulled them through mud just to see the tracks they made. They were part of a kid's life.

I received a red wagon for Christmas when I was three years old. Soon my wagon and I were inseparable. One time Ma even took her box camera down from the clock shelf and took a picture of me with my wagon. I was wearing bib overalls, a straw hat, a wide grin, and was holding tightly to the wagon's handle.

I hauled everything in my wagon: small stones, hunks of oat straw, ears of corn, pieces of stovewood, and my teddy bear that Ma had made from a feed sack. She told me I couldn't say wagon very clearly. I called my little red

transportation system a "waget." Where the wagon went I went. We could not be separated. It was if the wagon handle had been attached to my arm. Jerry and his waget.

One time I lost my wagon for a higher purpose. Pa didn't say it quite that way, but I knew what he meant. The wheelbarrow used for hauling milk cans from the barn to the milk house broke. Pa started using my wagon to haul milk cans. I was happy I could help out by lending him my wagon but soon realized that I no longer could use it when I wanted. My red wagon stood by the barn, ready to haul milk cans twice a day.

Finally, the regular milk-toting wheelbarrow was back in service, and the red wagon was mine again. It had a few more dents, and the rim was caved in a little when a filled milk can slipped and hit it, but mostly it was the same little red wagon that I had come to love so much.

As the years passed, I grew older and bigger and my wagon grew old and rusty. One day the front wheel fell off. Pa said it couldn't be fixed. "You're too old for a wagon, anyway," he said. I began wishing for a bicycle.

History of Little Red Wagons

Antonio Pasin began manufacturing children's Radio Flyer wagons in 1917. He had come to the United States in 1914 from Italy and handcrafted toy wooden wagons in a small rented shop, building them at night and trying to sell them during the day. Children loved his wooden wagons, but following his handcrafted approaches, he couldn't keep up with demand.

Meanwhile Pasin was watching the fledgling automobile industry. He was especially interested in how Henry Ford mass-produced Model-T autos, and he soon began making red metal wagons. By 1930 Pasin's company, Radio Steel & Manufacturing, had become the country's leading manufacturer of coaster wagons. Even during the Depression years, Pasin's company produced more than 1,500 wagons a day.

Pasin named his most popular coaster wagon the *Radio Flyer*. He was impressed with fellow Italian Guglielmo Marconi's invention of the radio. And he was likewise fascinated by the idea of airplanes and flight. During World War II, the Radio Flyer Company couldn't get steel for wagons and couldn't find enough labor to make them. During those years they manufactured the famous

"Blitz Can," a steel five-gallon fuel container that was strapped to the backs of jeeps, trucks, and tanks.

After the war the company returned to making coaster wagons. By the 1990s the Radio Flyer Company had become the world's leading producer of toy wagons. A third generation of Pasins runs the company today.

Sleds

People called them coaster sleds, hand sleighs, toy sleighs, and just plain sleds. It didn't matter what they were called. Come winter and the first snowstorm, kids found their sleds and went sledding.

It was the week following Thanksgiving, and it had snowed six inches, enough for sledding on the hill behind the Chain O' Lake school. I dragged my old sled down from the storage place above the woodshed, ran some sandpaper along the rusty runners, and headed for school. I knew that during first recess we'd all be out on the hill, those of us with cheap hardware store sleds, and Mildred, with her Flexible Flyer.

Flexible Flyers were the Cadillac of sleds. We all wanted a Flexible Flyer but knew we'd probably never get one. Sometimes, when Mildred Swen was in a good mood, she would let one of us ride down the hill with her, to get the feel for high-quality sledding on the back of her wonderful sled. What a thrill it was to ride on such a marvelous machine, to feel the wind rushing by, to hear the runners crunching on the hard-packed snow, to see the look of awe on the faces of your fellow schoolmates when you flew by. Then, as you approached the bottom of the hill, you felt this precision machine turn in a wide arc in one direction and then in the other. No other sled came close to riding as well as a Flexible Flyer, or so we believed. If the truth be known, there wasn't a wit of difference between the ride on a cheap hardware store sled or a Flexible Flyer.

It was clear, though, that the Flexible Flyer was better constructed and flashier to look at. The owners of

Flexible Flyer sleds also made sure we all knew the kind of sled they owned. That was clearly one of the important qualities of a Flexible Flyer. It gave a kid bragging rights.

History of Sleds

Sledding has been popular since Colonial days, when children slid down hills with wooden sleds. The best wooden sleds had wooden runners to which a strip of metal had been attached to make the sled move faster. But these sleds couldn't be steered, not much anyway. The rider went where the sled went, through berry patches and into trees.

The Flexible Flyer was the first sled that could be steered. Samuel Leeds Allen, a farm equipment manufacturer in the late 1800s, discovered that he needed a product that could be made in summer and sold in winter to keep his employees working when the machinery manufacturing business was slow. In 1889 he designed the Flexible Flyer sled.

Allen tried various sled designs. Eventually he replaced wooden runners with flexible steel ones. By attaching a movable crossbar, the sled became steerable. He named his creation, Flexible Flyer and added the now famous arrow and eagle design to the slatted wooden seat so everyone could recognize his creation.

Like so many new ideas, department stores and other retailers were reluctant to stock this new-fangled sled. It took nearly five years before it caught on. But with increased interest in tobogganing and ice-skating, Flexible Flyer sales increased dramatically. Allen's new sled soon sold more than all the other sled manufacturers combined.

The Flexible Flyer sled is still a prestigious sled. It has maintained its reputation over the years and today is a reminder of not only the fun of sliding downhill, but how, no matter what kids had, they longed for the Cadillac of sleds.

Ice-Fishing Shanties

Some people look at the Midwest with its long, cold winters and wonder how those who live there can survive. Ice fishing and ice shanties are a way for Northern people to stare winter in the face and enjoy what they see, a way to be outside yet have an escape from harsh weather.

It was a Saturday morning in late November and it was cold. The thermometer on the back porch read ten below zero three days in a row but today it was a tad warmer, only zero.

"It's time to go ice fishing, boys," Pa said to my two brothers and me. "Ice ought be in good shape by now." By that he meant the ice on the area lakes had frozen to a thickness that would support people walking on it and would also support a fish shanty.

Starting that day, we would ice fish every weekend throughout the middle of winter and every day during the

two-week Christmas school break. All that would keep us off the ice was a blizzard or brutally cold weather when the thermometer dipped lower than twenty below at night and didn't creep above ten below during the day.

My brothers and I helped load our ice-fishing shanty on the back of our 1950 Chevy pickup. The ice shanty was no prize. It had once been six inches taller, but several years ago an extended thaw in February created several inches of slush on the lake and the shanty sank a few inches into the ice. When the temperature dropped again, the ice shanty froze and we had to saw off the bottom to move it from the lake. It was against the law to leave an ice shanty on a lake beyond a certain date. I suspect the sawed-off floor eventually floated to shore somewhere. We didn't look for it.

With a new floor in the ice shanty, we had to hunch over to get into it. Once inside, if you forgot and stood up quickly, you cracked your head on the metal roof. Our shanty was about six feet square with windows on three sides and bench seats fastened to the walls. A small sheet metal stove, on short legs, stood in one corner of the shack, nailed to the floor so that it stayed in place. A discarded rain downspout served as a chimney. An entry door was located near the stove. And that was it. Nothing fancy.

Our shanty required us to run outside when a fish bit— when a tip-up flag flew up announcing that a northern pike or a black bass had come by and grabbed our bait. If we wanted to fish panfish with a jig pole, a small fishing pole we hand-held, we sat on a pail outside the shanty. When we got cold, we snuck inside.

For us, ice fishing was more than catching fish. There was the beauty of a winter day. Some days were cloud-free with the low winter sun creating long shadows and sparkling snowfields. On such days the ice often talked. As it contracted, it cracked, sending long fissures in every direction. Cracking ice created spectacular sounds that echoed through the valley around the lake. At times the sound was a soft groan or a low rumbling. Occasionally it was sharper and louder, a sound of protest on a quiet day.

One year we brought our wind-up record player from home and played John Phillip Sousa marches and other inspiring music while we fished. We also had Gene Autry singing "You Are My Sunshine" that we mixed in with the Sousa marches to add variety to our cultural experience.

Our fish shanty was one among about a dozen on the lake. We arrived around ten in the morning, after the farm chores were done. After starting the fire in our shanty stove, we settled in for a day of fishing and storytelling.

Unless it was bitterly cold, we were outside the shanty comparing fish stories with other fishermen and waiting for our tip-ups to fly up. On a good day we might have three or four tip-ups, sometimes more, but often fewer. Some days we'd sit from 10:00 in the morning until 4:00 in the afternoon and catch nothing.

Inside, the shanty was either too hot or too cold. When the wood in the little stove was snapping and crackling, it was too hot inside. When it sputtered, sizzled, and smoked, we froze. But no one complained. The good qualities of ice fishing shanties far outnumbered their miserable qualities.

History of Ice-Fishing Shanties

Ice-fishing shanties have been around as long as ice fishermen have. The earliest ones were crude, wooden affairs built to keep the fishermen out of the wind. As the years passed, shanties became fancier. Wood-burning stoves, and later bottled gas stoves, were added. Picture windows became common. TV sets and radios were installed. And shanties became larger. Eventually, many were so comfortable that fisherman never ventured outside but sat inside with the ice holes within the shanty. But with all the amenities, the ice-fishing shanty for many true Northerners was merely an excuse to venture outside and face winter and share a day on the ice with a friend.

Card Playing

Before television, when winter arrived, many farm families got together and played cards on long, cold evenings. Most rural people had learned one or two card games when they were growing up and continued playing once or twice a month starting in late November. Playing cards was fun, but for most farm families, it a was a chance to visit, swap stories, and catch up on the neighborhood news.

I knew something was going to happen because Ma was dusting in the dining room, cleaning off the big oak table, and even polishing the shiny parts of the wood heater.

"Preacher coming?" I asked.

"No, Millers are coming over tonight to play cards."

Ma had baked a chocolate cake and made a batch of bologna sandwiches that she'd covered with a dish towel.

The topic of conversation at the supper table was the upcoming card game and how the men had beat the women the last time they played, three games to one.

"We shoulda won them all," Pa said.

"You sure you didn't cheat?" he said to Ma, with a twinkle in his eye.

"You know I don't cheat," she answered. We all knew that card playing was a serious matter for Ma. You didn't tease her about it, but Pa usually did anyway.

I wasn't old enough to play regularly, only once in awhile when I sat in for someone. Even when I couldn't play, I liked to watch and listen.

About seven-thirty, Bill and Lorraine Miller arrived. They had walked; everyone did in those days. Once they had a chance to warm up by the stove, they arranged themselves around the oak dining room table, men across from each other, same for the women.

Ma explained that the reason the women lost the last time they played was that the cards were wornout and sticky. She had gotten a new deck of shiny, slippery cards that she shuffled and dealt around the table.

Soon the bidding began.

"I bid three," said Lorraine.

"Pass," said Bill.

"Four," said Pa.

"I can't bid," Ma said.

And the game began. I could see that Pa was going to make four easily and probably all six, the maximum bid in smear, the game they were playing.

The next round, Ma bid four and didn't make it. I heard her grumbling under her breath. The worst thing for Ma was to bid and not make it; that was even worse than being dealt bad cards. She figured that most of the time she had bad cards, and that's why she couldn't win.

As the evening went on, the men won all the games. In only one game did the women even come close and then the score was twenty-one to sixteen. When the last game was finished, Ma got up to pour coffee and pass the bologna sandwiches and chocolate cake that she'd cut in huge squares.

Bill Miller, knowing full well how serious Ma was about the game and how she hated losing, said, "Say, Eleanor, what happened to those new cards you bought? Thought they were gonna make the difference."

"I think you men cheat," Ma said, without the hint of a smile.

Bill dropped the topic, and soon he and Lorraine were on their way home. Ma and Pa didn't say much to each other as they gathered up the dirty dishes and carried them to the kitchen. There were times when even Pa knew enough to keep his mouth shut.

History of Card Playing

Rural people have played cards for years. They played in church basements, backrooms of taverns, American Legion halls, deer hunting camps, ice-fishing shanties, and farm homes.

Common card games besides smear included: euchre, sheepshead (schafskopf), gin rummy, pinochle, cribbage, and several poker games such as five-card and seven-card stud. Some regions have their own special games; in German communities it is often smear. In many places, euchre is the game of choice. The Midvalers group at Midvale Community Lutheran Church in Madison, Wisconsin, sponsors a euchre night each year that attracts a room full of card players.

Besides regular card playing at taverns, churches, and other sites, many families played cards at holiday gatherings, anniversaries, and birthdays. Although less popular today, card playing has survived and may even be on the increase.

Polka Bands

Polka bands have been popular in the Midwest since the immigrants brought their love for polka music and their playing skills from the old country. For many older people, the sound of a polka band takes them back to their youth, to the days when dance halls were everywhere and people danced the polka every Saturday night, the year around.

I remember the first wedding dance I attended. The dance hall was on Fish Lake, a low-ceilinged building with a bar on one side and a restaurant on the other. The dance floor was in the center with a few tables and chairs scattered around the edges, a place for the watchers— those too timid to dance, those too old to dance more than a few rounds, and those who liked the music but couldn't dance a step.

On one end of the floor was a stage, maybe only a couple feet higher than the rest of the floor but high enough so that the band was above the dancers. Tickets were fifty cents. The attendant stamped my hand at the door with near-permanent ink so I could go outside to cool off or could walk in the moonlight by the lake. This was what the older boys were doing, I later noticed. I didn't know why they'd want to miss any of the polka music and the dancing.

Couples and singles began streaming into the dance hall shortly before nine, women wearing skirts and blouses, men wearing pants and open shirts, and everyone wearing comfortable shoes for hopping and sliding, which is what I decided polka dancing was all about. I watched the dance hall owner sprinkle the floor with dance-floor wax.

Promptly at nine the band tuned up. It was the Sunset Ramblers. I'd heard Pa talk about them, that they were a family band organized by Clifford Banks and his wife. Clifford played the guitar and banjo. His wife played an accordion. One son played trumpet, another a bass violin.

They started off with the "Beer Barrel Polka", one that everyone knew and loved. Then the "Pennsylvania Polka" and the "Clarinet Polka". Three polkas, three old-time waltzes, a couple of schottisches, a flying Dutchman, and a circle two-step. I had to ask what the various dances were.

Someone requested the "Butcher Song." I thought that a strange name for a polka. Then the band began playing and singing "Butcher arms around me honey, hold me tight."

Then someone yelled, "How about the 'Too Fat Polka?'" The band went immediately to singing, "I don't want her, you can have her, she's too fat for me."

Finally, the band played a slow dance, a draggy kind of step for the boys who couldn't handle the polka but who could now move around the dance floor with their dates. I noticed some of the older polka dancers were out there, too, welcoming a chance to catch their breath and restore the feeling in their legs.

Lorraine Miller came over and asked if I wanted to dance. I said I'd rather watch. What I really meant was I didn't have the first idea about how to dance. But I knew I was going to learn.

I saw smiles everywhere. Worries and concerns seemed to disappear, evaporating like rainwater on hot rocks. I noticed that some of the girls were dragging their shy boyfriends onto the dance floor, trying to show them how to polka and waltz, how to move around the floor with the music. Girls had learned these skills from their mothers or older sisters. Many of the boys came to the dance with two left feet and a desire to dance, but no skill. Some couldn't even keep the beat. I guessed the only beat they knew was that of a John Deere tractor or the "ka bang," "ka bang," of a hay baler.

Wedding dances like this one were special. It was a chance to see the wedding party and poke fun at the groom and eat a big free lunch besides. I couldn't wait until I was old enough to go to polka dances by myself.

History of Polka Bands

Polka dancing and polka music came to the Midwest with the immigrants, with the Germans and the Poles, with the Norwegians and the Slovenians, with the Czechs and the Finns, the Swiss and the Irish, the Belgians and the Italians. Each group brought a slightly different version of the polka, a special sound that tied the music to their European heritage.

Polka bands continue to be popular at wedding dances, anniversaries, and at special polka festivals. Polka bands bring people together for fun and celebration and offer them an opportunity to take their minds off serious matters, at least for a couple of hours.

Back Porches

Back porches on farm homes were gathering places where families met at the end of the day, where neighbors visited, where the eggs were cleaned, where stovewood was stored, and where the farm dog rested.

The western sky was a collage of reds, pinks, and purples as the late June sun slipped below the horizon and the coolness of evening began settling over the land. Fingers of mist rose from the valleys, and the last robin sang its evening song.

In the distance I heard a cowbell, a signal that the neighbor's cows were grazing in their night pasture on the long hillside that we could see from our farmyard, but dimly as the evening light slowly gave way to darkness.

We gathered on the back porch after the evening milking, Pa, Ma, my two brothers, and I. We talked about the day, about the hay crop, about the corn and how well it was coming up, about the oats and how well they were growing, about the hay mower that needed replacing one of these years.

It was nearly dark now; a dim light came from a lone kerosene lamp sitting in the middle of the kitchen table, a quiet yellow beacon. Fireflies skittered here and there, specks of cold light that came on strong and then trailed off, like tiny flashlights with wings and no direction, or so it seemed.

We talked quietly. Pa shared a story about an earlier

time when he was a lad and his family was making hay, wild hay, for his father hadn't known about alfalfa and red clover. Pa told about cutting hay with horses, about raking it and piling it into bunches to dry and then hauling it to the cow barn with a steel-wheeled wagon and pitching it into the haymow. By hand. With a three-tine pitchfork.

I thought about the fact that his story took place forty years ago and we still made hay in almost the same way, with horses, with three-tine pitchforks, with a steel-wheeled wagon.

We sat quietly for a time, no one saying anything. Then we heard it, the whippoorwill in the field back of the house, near the strawberry patch and not far from the woods. It repeated again and again "Plant your corn, plant your corn." That's what Pa said the bird was calling; Ma said the bird cried "Whip poor Will." We had a neighbor named Will, so the call was personal but inappropriate because Will was a good guy. We counted the calls, five, ten, sometimes twenty in a row before the bird stopped. In the distance we heard an answer, another whippoorwill calling, "Whip poor Will." Were these messages of love? Probably, but we didn't talk about such things. We just listened to those night birds call to each other and to us, and we enjoyed the sound.

Ma said that Uncle Charlie and Aunt Sophie were coming to the farm for a couple of weeks in July for their annual vacation. Pa remembered how Uncle Charlie always complained about the whippoorwill, that it kept him awake at night. Pa didn't like Uncle Charlie, said that he complained about everything and besides that he was lazy. "You gotta put up a stick to see if he's moving," Pa said about Uncle Charlie.

Stars were everywhere in the summer sky, little candles flickering in a gigantic expanse of nothingness. They extended from horizon to horizon, big ones and little ones, dim ones and bright ones, those that flickered and those that were steady—great mysteries all.

From the hayfield in front of the house, the field that we mowed that afternoon, we smelled the sweet aroma of alfalfa and sweet clover drifting quietly on the night air, tantalizing us with a perfume that has never been equaled by the finest perfume makers in the world. At least that was the thinking of country folk who had a chance to smell mown hay.

Pa dug his pocket watch from his bib overalls and held it up to catch a glimmer of light from the kitchen lamp. "About nine," he reported. "Time for bed. Sunup before you know it."

We all filed into the house and to bed. The smell of new-mown hay drifted through my bedroom window, and I heard the whippoorwill calling again and again as I drifted off to sleep.

References
(in order by chapter)

Lamps and Lanterns

Katherine C. Grier *Kerosene Era, 1860-1900, Part II*, Rochester, NY: Strong Museum, 1985.

W.T. Kirkman. "Kerosene Lanterns," www.lanternnet.com

Silos

Jerry Apps. *Barns of Wisconsin*, Madison, WI: Wisconsin Trails, 1995.

Jerry Apps. *Cheese: The Making of a Wisconsin Tradition*, Amherst, WI: Amherst Press, 1998.

Walking Plows

"John Deere: Our History: The Story of John Deere," www.deere.com, history section.

Joseph J. Schroeder, Jr. *Sears, Roebuck & Company, 1908 Catalogue*, Chicago, IL: Gun Digest Company, 1969.

Windmills

Jerry Apps. *Mills of Wisconsin and the Midwest*, Madison, WI: Tamarack Press, 1980, pp. 94-96.

Joseph J. Schroeder, Jr. *Sears, Roebuck & Company, 1908 Catalogue*, Chicago, IL: Gun Digest Company, 1969.

Gasoline Engines

"Briggs & Stratton History," www.briggsandstratton.com, history section.

"Fairbanks Morse Engine Technology, 1880s," www.xnet.com

Tractors

Henry Rasmussen. *International McCormick Tractors*, Osceola, WI: Motorbooks International, 1989.

Robert N. Pripps. *Great American Farm Tractors*, Ann Arbor, MI: Lowe & B. Hould, 1998.

Robert N. Pripps. *Ford Tractors*, Osceola, WI: Motorbooks International, 1990.

Threshing Machines

Harris Pearson Smith. *Farm Machinery and Equipment*, New York: McGraw-Hill, 1948.

Robert N. Pripps. *Threshers: History of the Separator Threshing Machine, Reaper, & Harvester*, Osceola, WI: Motorbooks International, 1992.

www.jicase.com, history section.

Barbed Wire Fences

Robert T. Clifton. *Barbs, Prongs, Points, Prickers, and Stickers: A Complete and Illustrated Catalogue of Antique Barbed Wire*, Norman, OK: University of Oklahoma, 1972.

Christopher Johnson. "Barbed Wire," *Concord Review*, Spring, 1990.

Rural Mail Carriers

www.usps.Gov

Telephones

Kate Dooner. *Telephones Antique to Modern*, West Chester, PA: Schiffer Publishing, Ltd., 1992.

Ralph Meyer. *Old Time Telephones: Technology, Restoration and Repair,* New York: McGraw Hill, Inc., 1994.

Mail-Order Catalogs

Joseph J. Schroeder, Jr. *Sears, Roebuck & Company 1908 Catalogue*, Chicago, IL: Gun Digest Company, 1969.

Wisconsin State Journal, January 26, 1993.

www.mward.com, www.sears.com, history section.

Box Cameras

George Gilbert. *Photography*, New York: Harper, 1980.

www.kodak.com, history section.

Radios

Paul H. Landis. "Radio on the Farm," *Rural Life in Process*, New York: McGraw-Hill Book Company, 1940.
"1895: Marconi's Invention," www.alpcom.it/hamradio/marconi.
"1920-1929—Early Broadcasting," www.northwinds.net/behris/1920.
"Old-Time Radio: The Golden Years," www.old-time.com/golden.

Country Taverns

James Leary. *Wisconsin Folklore*, Madison, WI: University of Wisconsin Press, 1999.

Gristmills

Jerry Apps. *Mills of Wisconsin and The Midwest*, Madison, WI: Wisconsin Trails, 1980.

Country Stores

April Halberstad. *Farm Memories: An Illustrated History of Rural Life*, Osceola, WI: Motorbooks International, 1996.
Paul H. Landis. *Rural Life in Process*, New York: McGraw-Hill Book Company, 1940.

4-H Clubs

Franklin M. Reck. *The 4-H Story: A History of 4-H Club Work*, Ames, IA: The Iowa State College Press, 1951.
Thomas Wessel and Marilyn Wessel. *4-H: An American Idea, 1900-1980*, Chevy Chase, MD: National 4-H Council, 1982.

County Fairs

Some information from Bob Williams, Coordinator of Fairs: Wisconsin Department of Agriculture, Trade and Consumer Protection.

Town Halls

"Township Government in The United States," www.schaumburgtownship.org

One-Room Country Schools

Jerry Apps. *One-Room Country Schools: History and Recollections From Wisconsin,* Amherst, WI: Amherst Press, 1996.

Little Red Wagons

www.radioflyer.com, history section.

Sleds

David Hoffman. *Kid Stuff: Great Toys From Our Childhood,* San Francisco: Chronicle Books, 1996.

Polka Bands

James Leary. *Wisconsin Folklore,* Madison, WI: University of Wisconsin Press, 1999.

Index